These Mandala's belong to the collection of

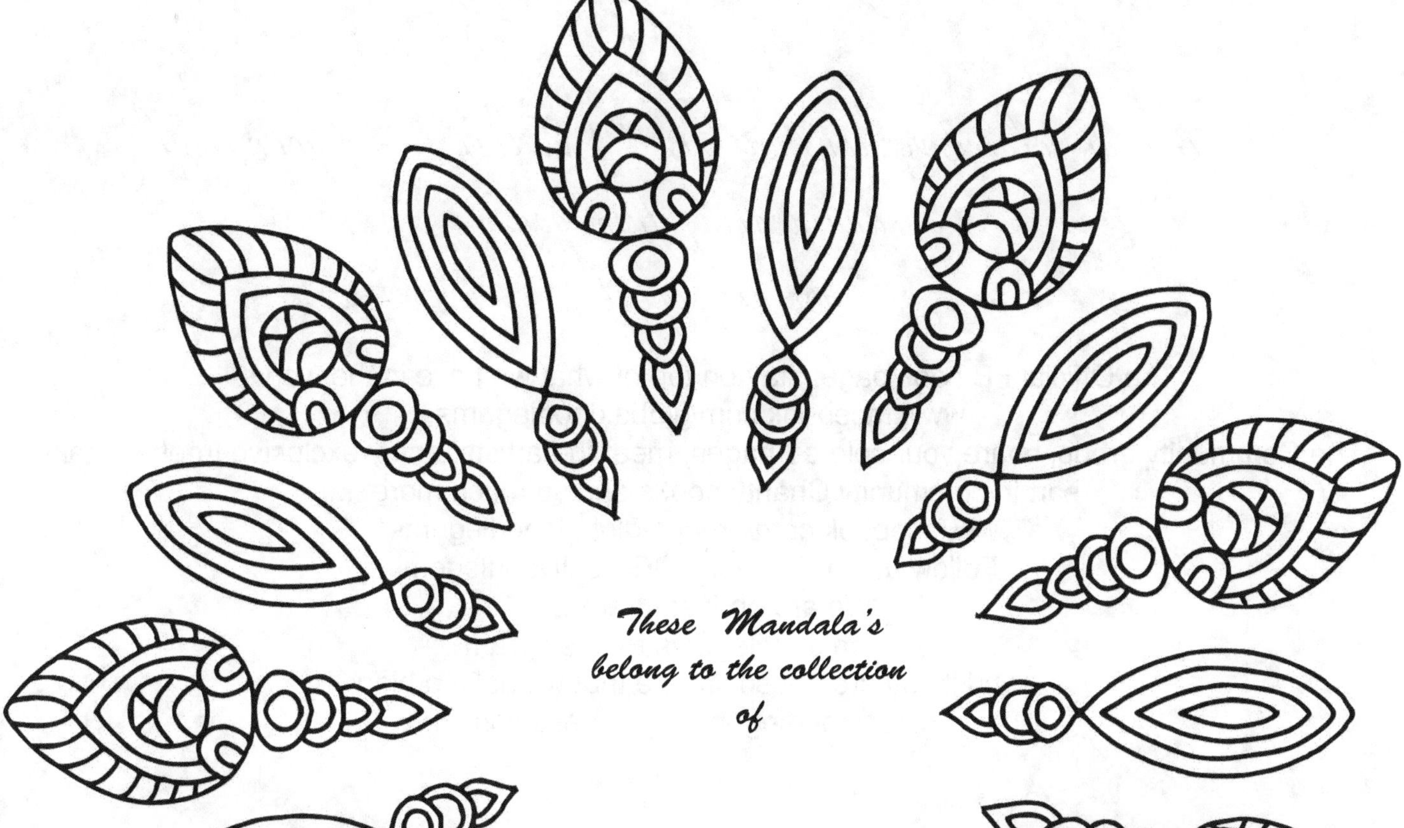

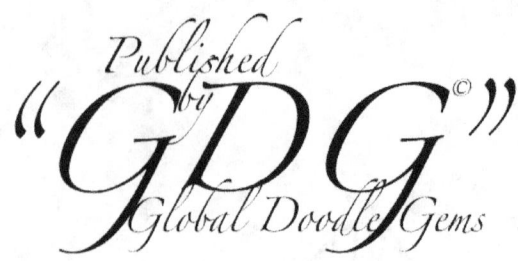

Share your colored versions with us! We love seeing your results and hearing from you we are social!

The Official FB book page, stay on top of what we have in the works!
www.facebook.com/globaldoodlegems
The Community group, share your colored pages, meet the artists, enjoy exclusive freebies, take part in community Charity books and so much more......
www.facebook.com/groups/globaldoodlegems/
Follow us on Twitter.... @GlobalDoodlegem
We are on Instagram too
@globaldoodlegems for instagram
...and if you are not social like that we have a blog
globaldoodlegems.wordpress.com

Copyright © 2017 Global Doodle Gems
All rights are reserved by Global Doodle Gems.
Duplication of pages for personal use are allowed. You are invited to color the pages then scan/post your coloured versions to social networks, mentioning the book title and author/artist (Global Doodle Gems).
All artwork and images are protected by copyright laws. This book or any portion thereof may not, otherwise, be reproduced and/or distributed or transmitted without the express written permission of the artist/publisher of Global Doodle Gems.
All of us from the Global Doodle Gems wish you a colortastic time and look forward to seeing your wonderful color results online!

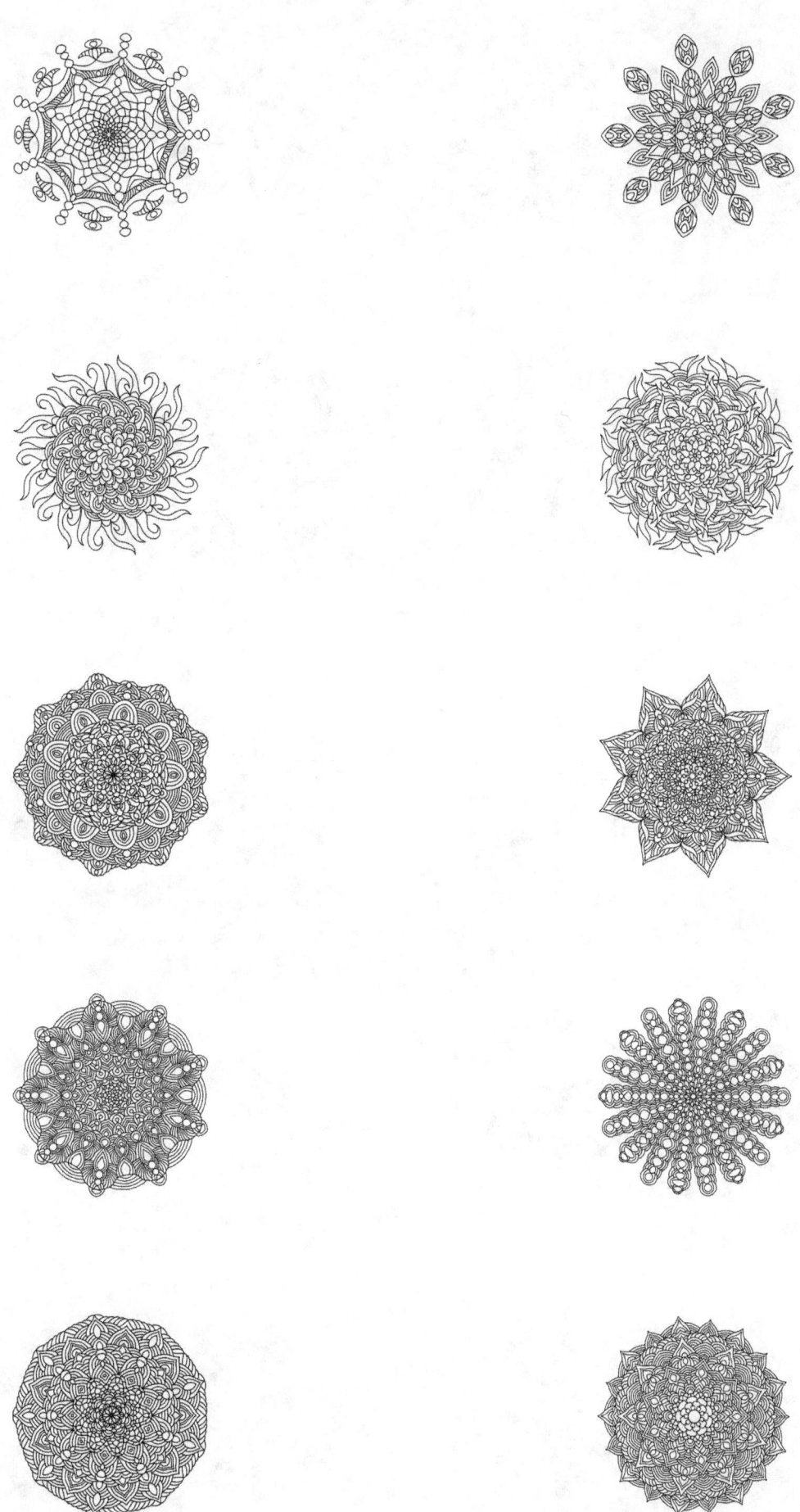

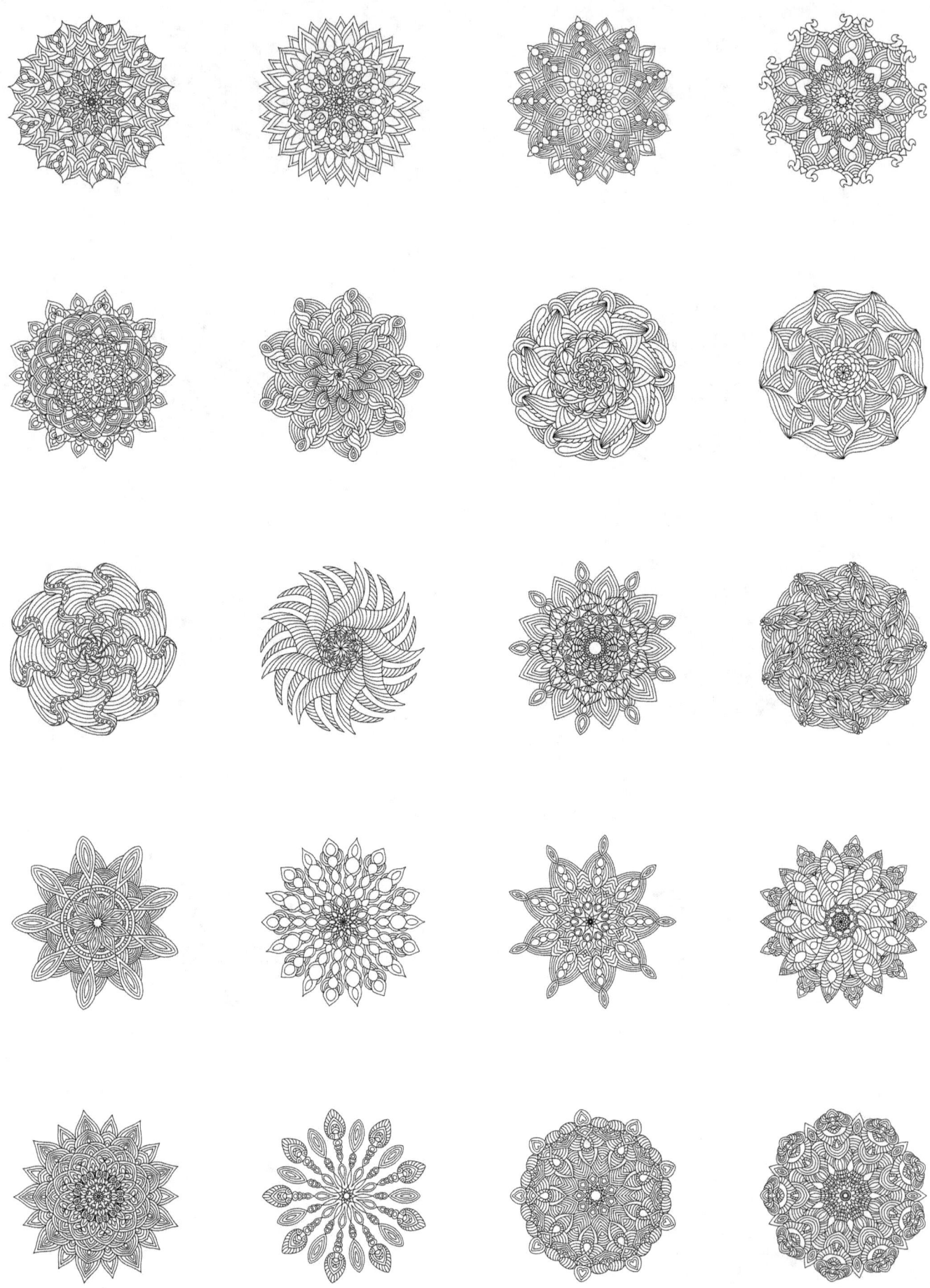

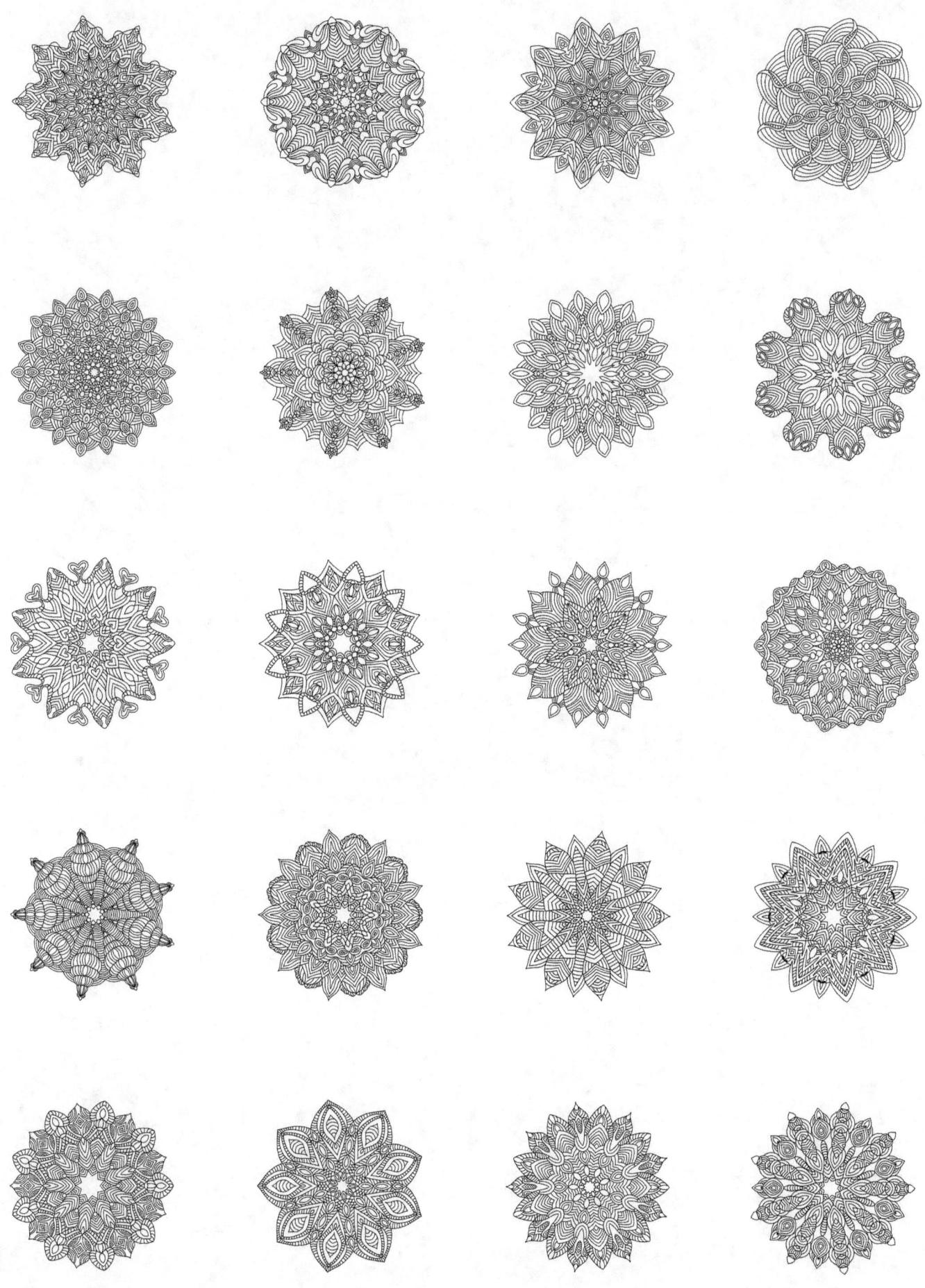

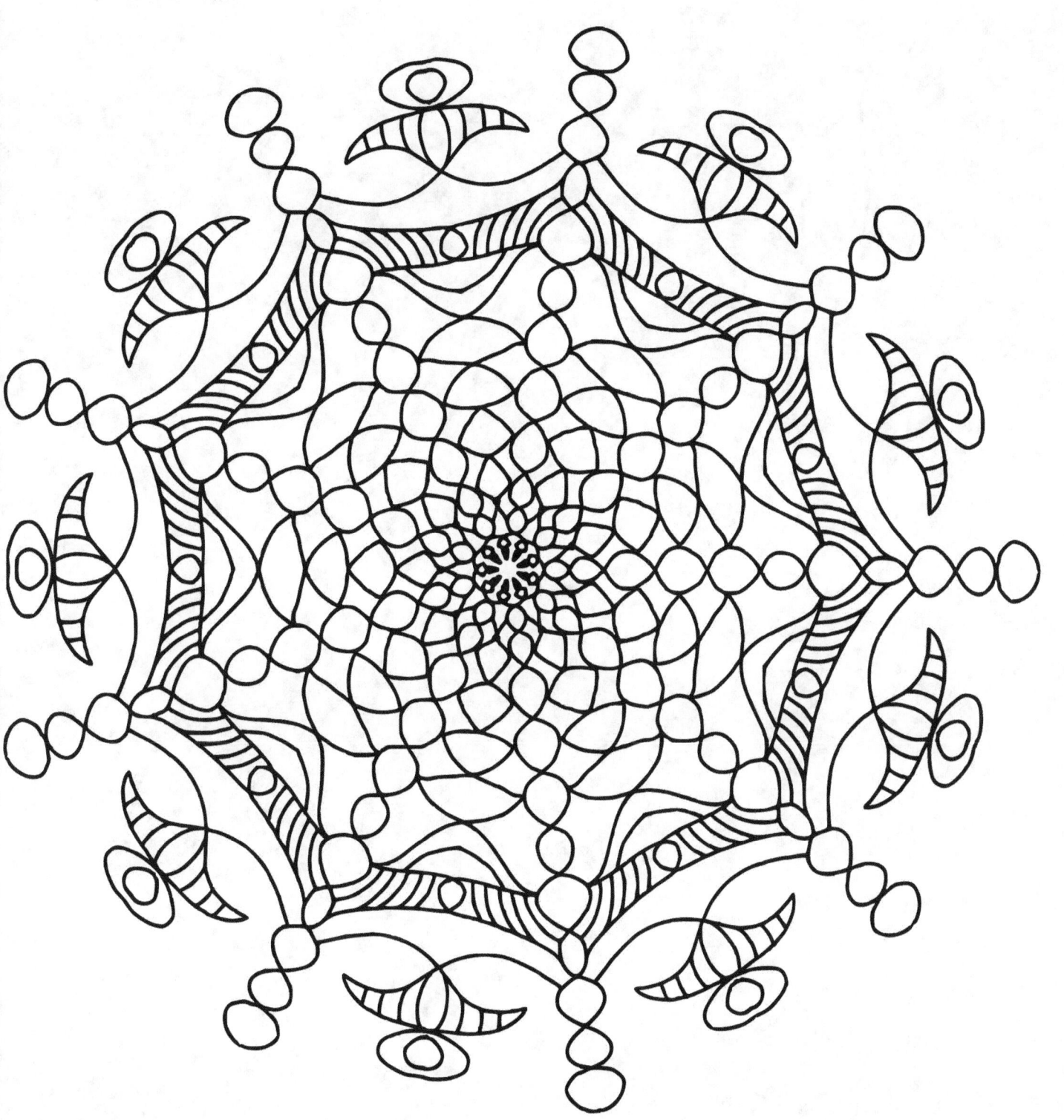

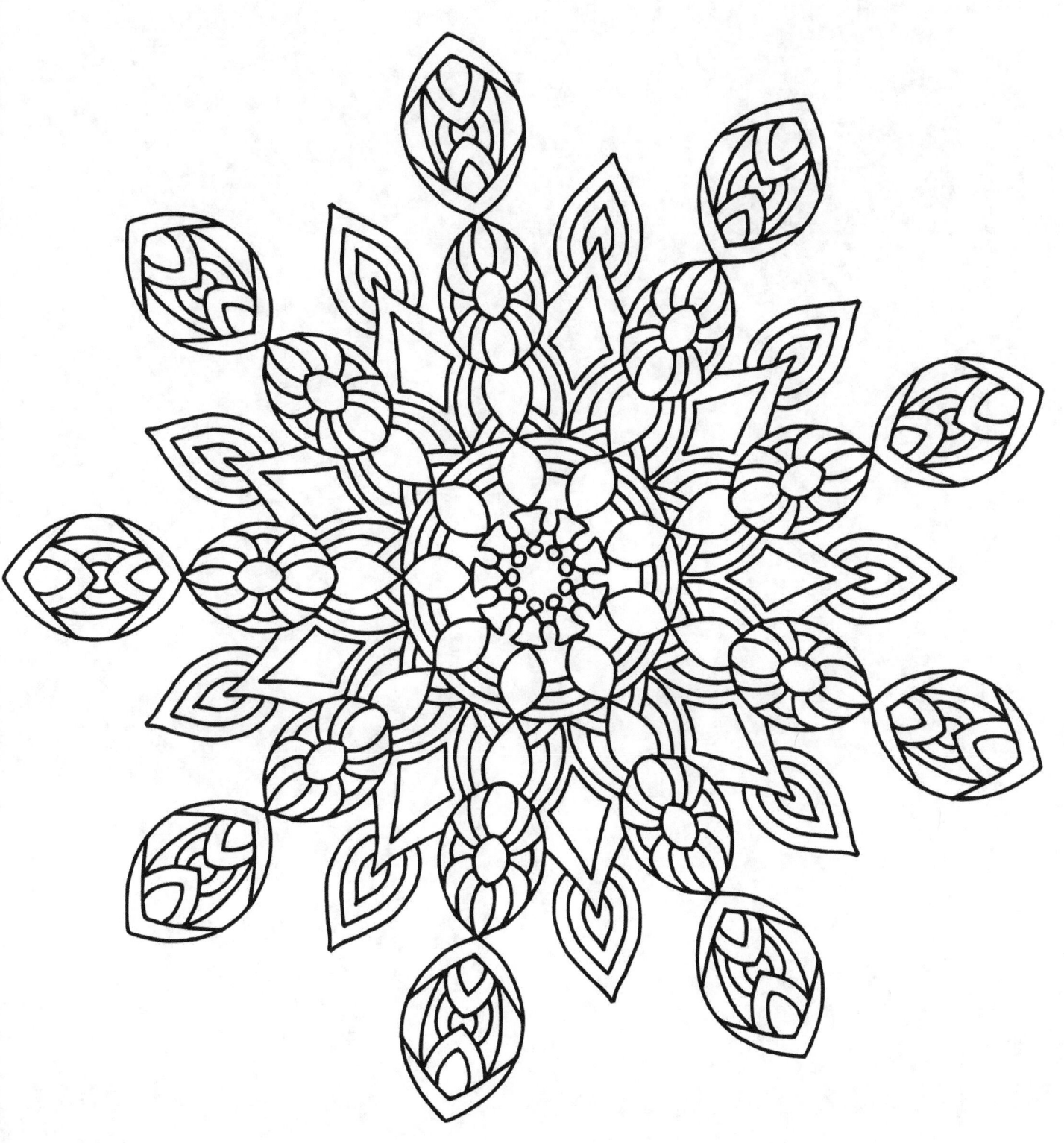

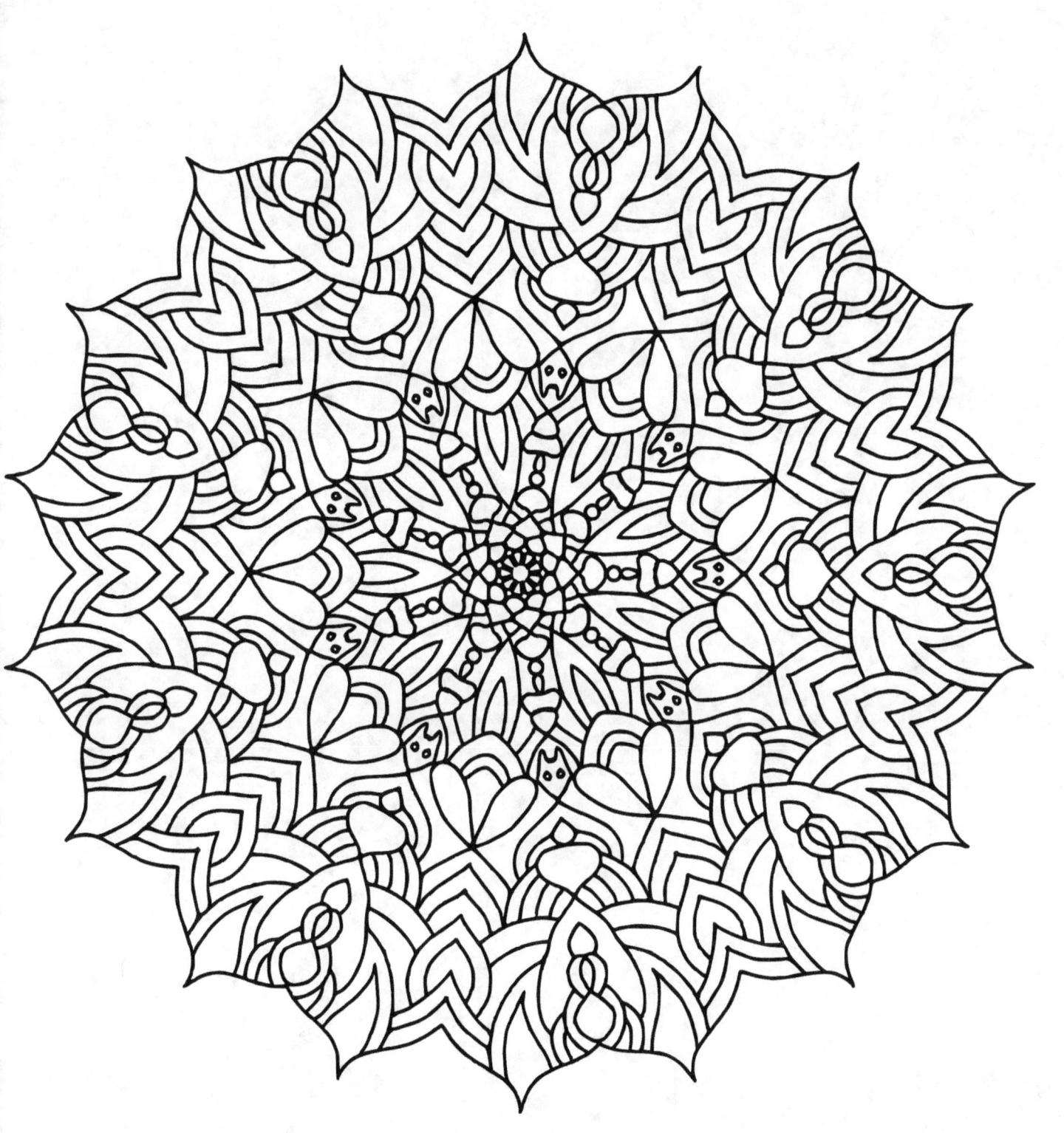

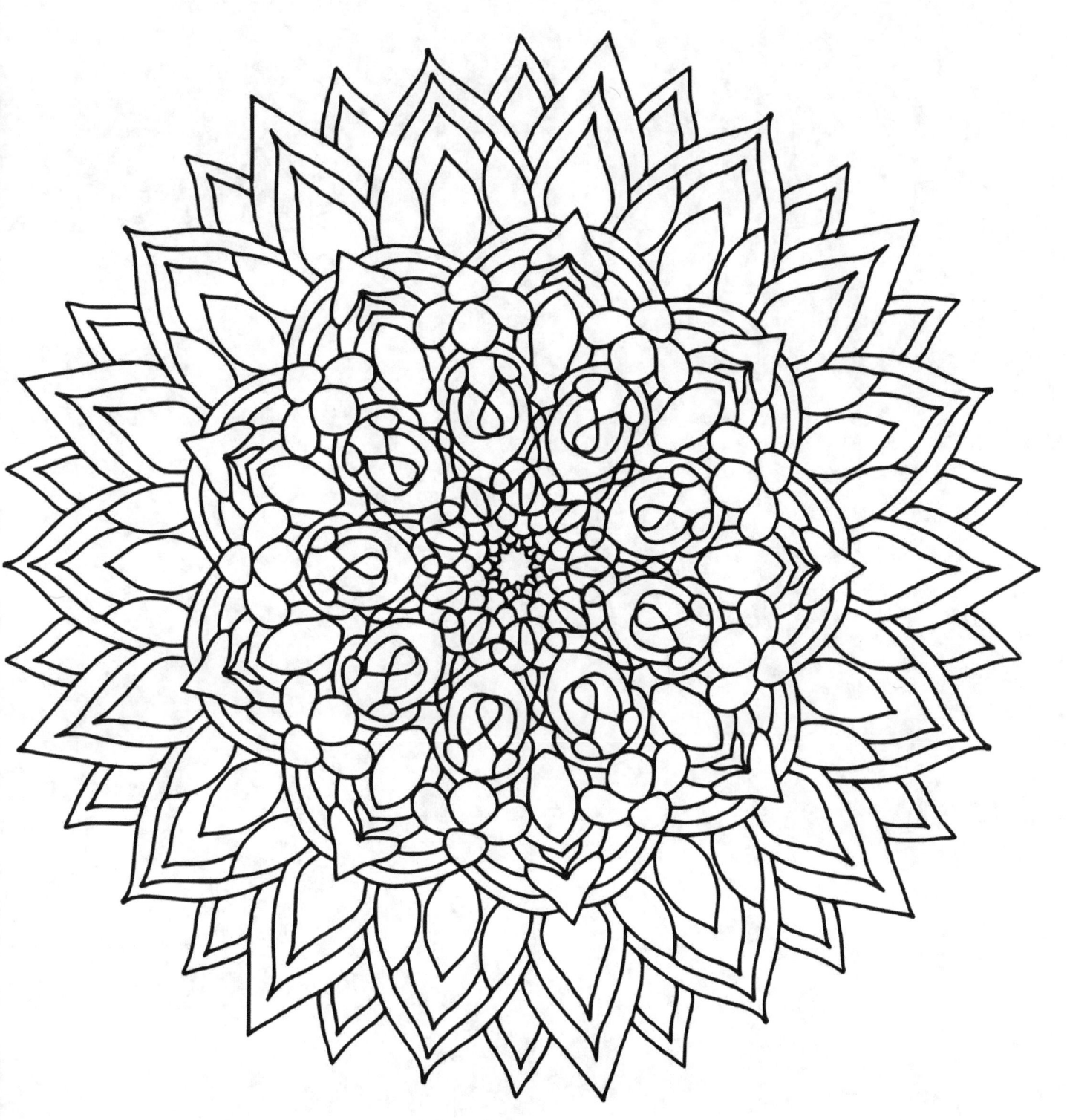

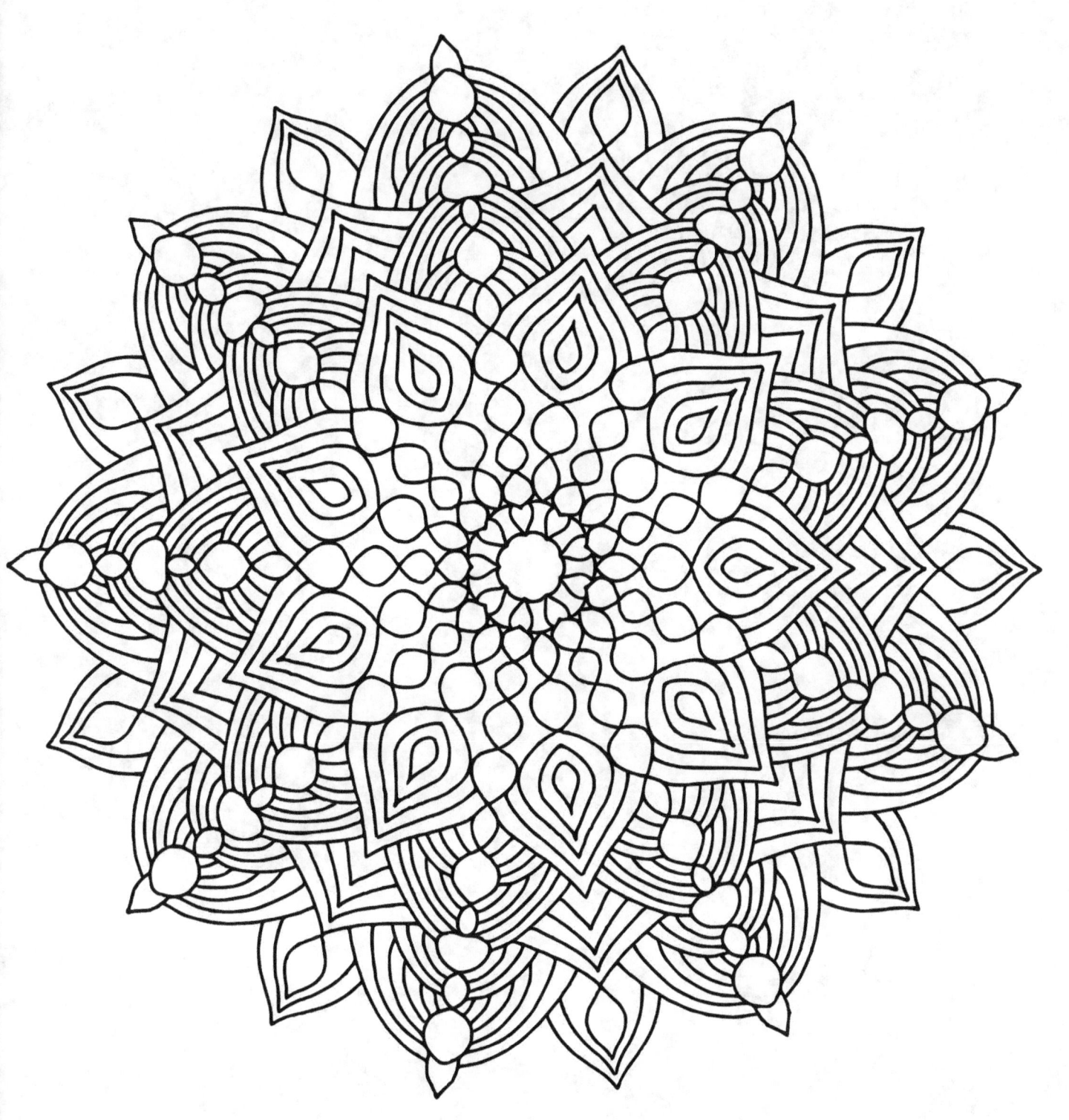

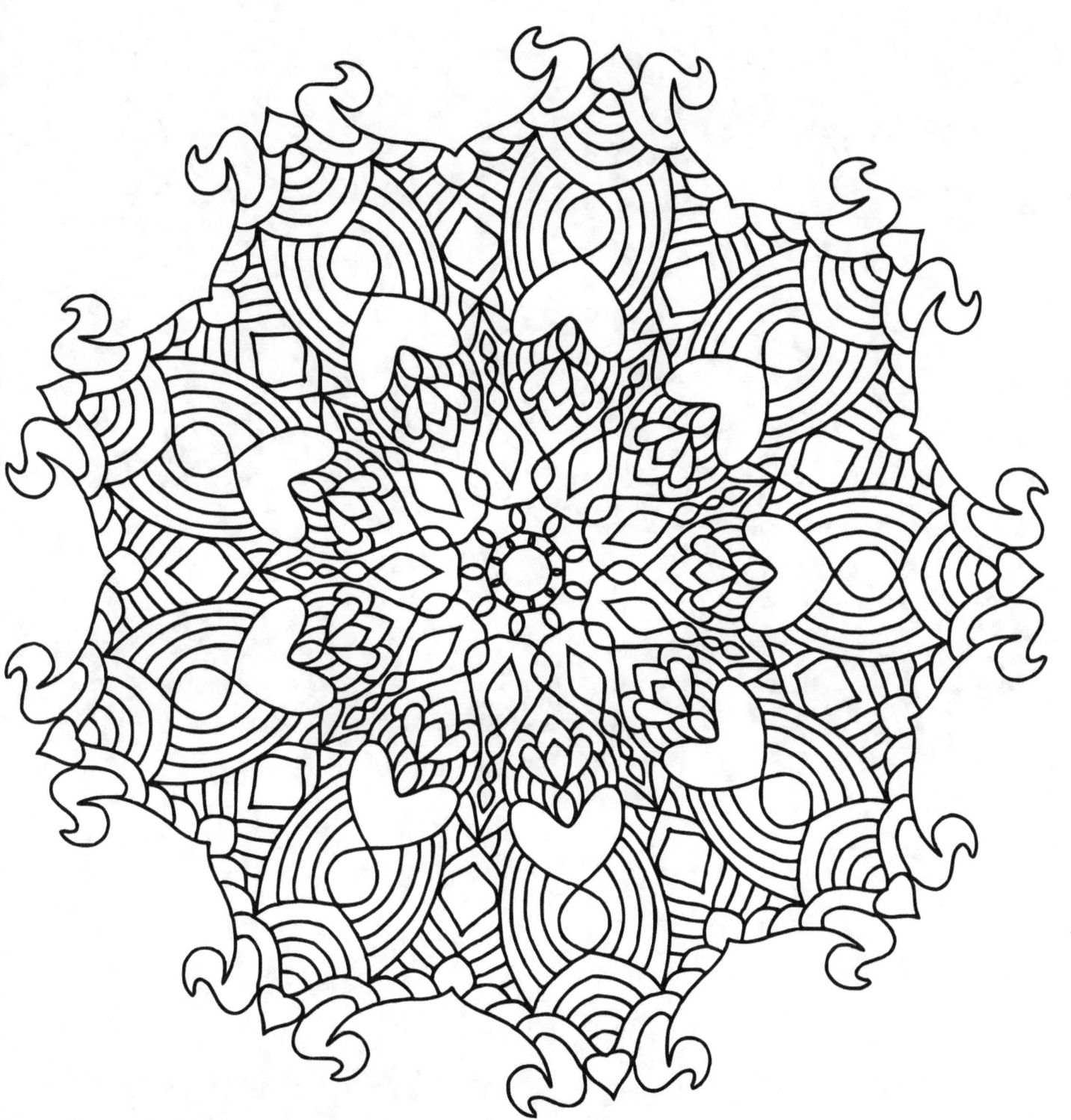

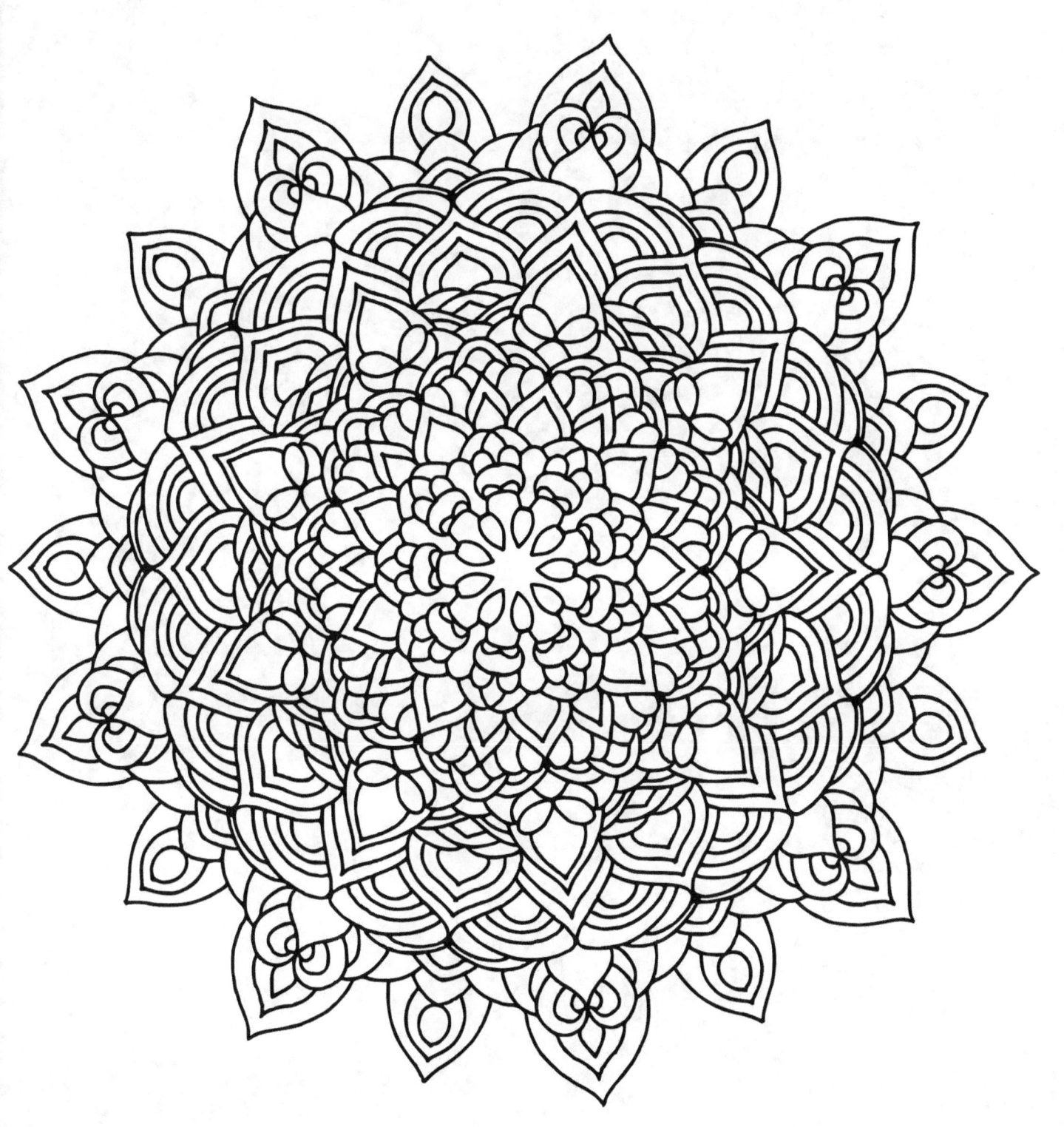

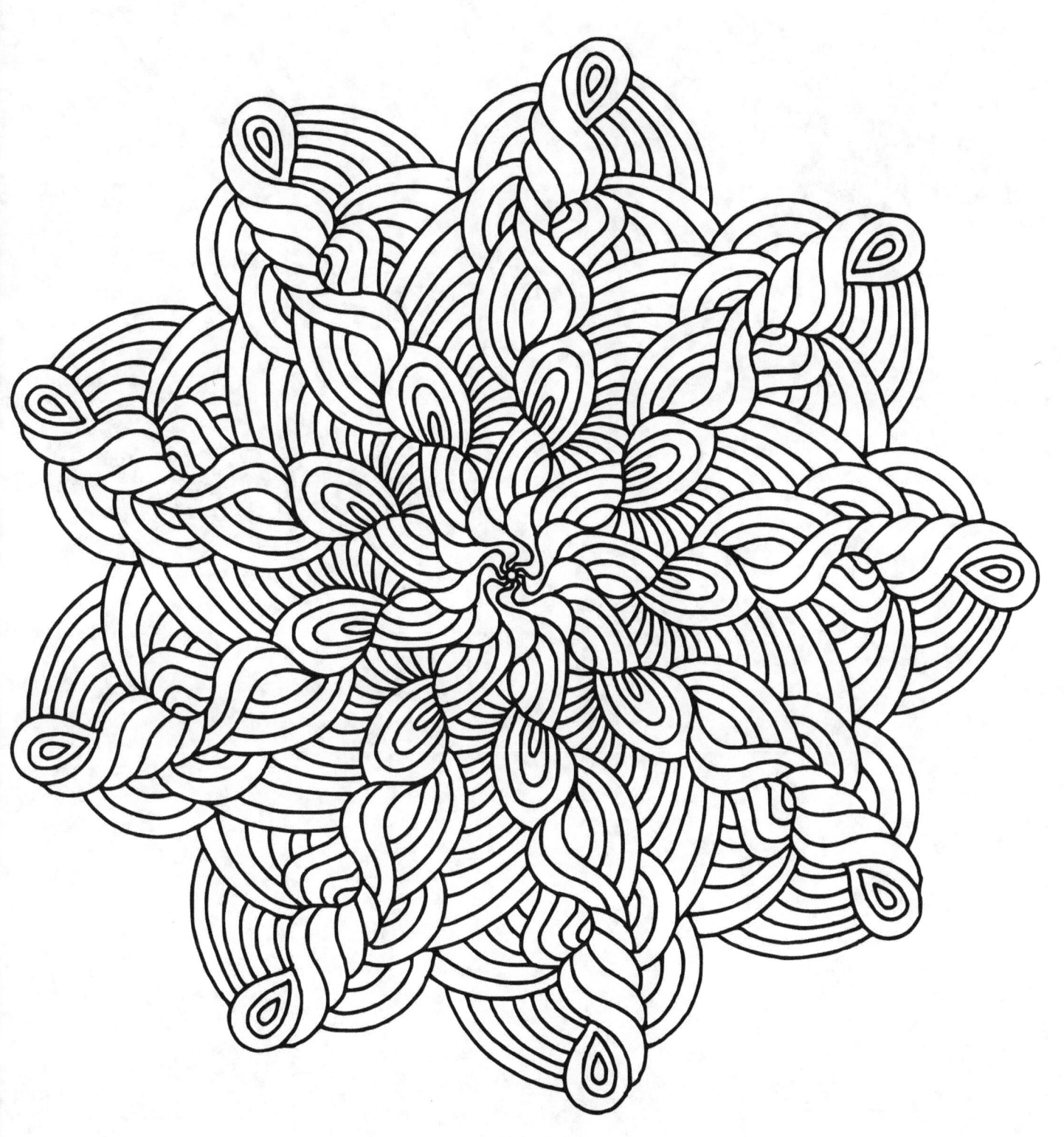

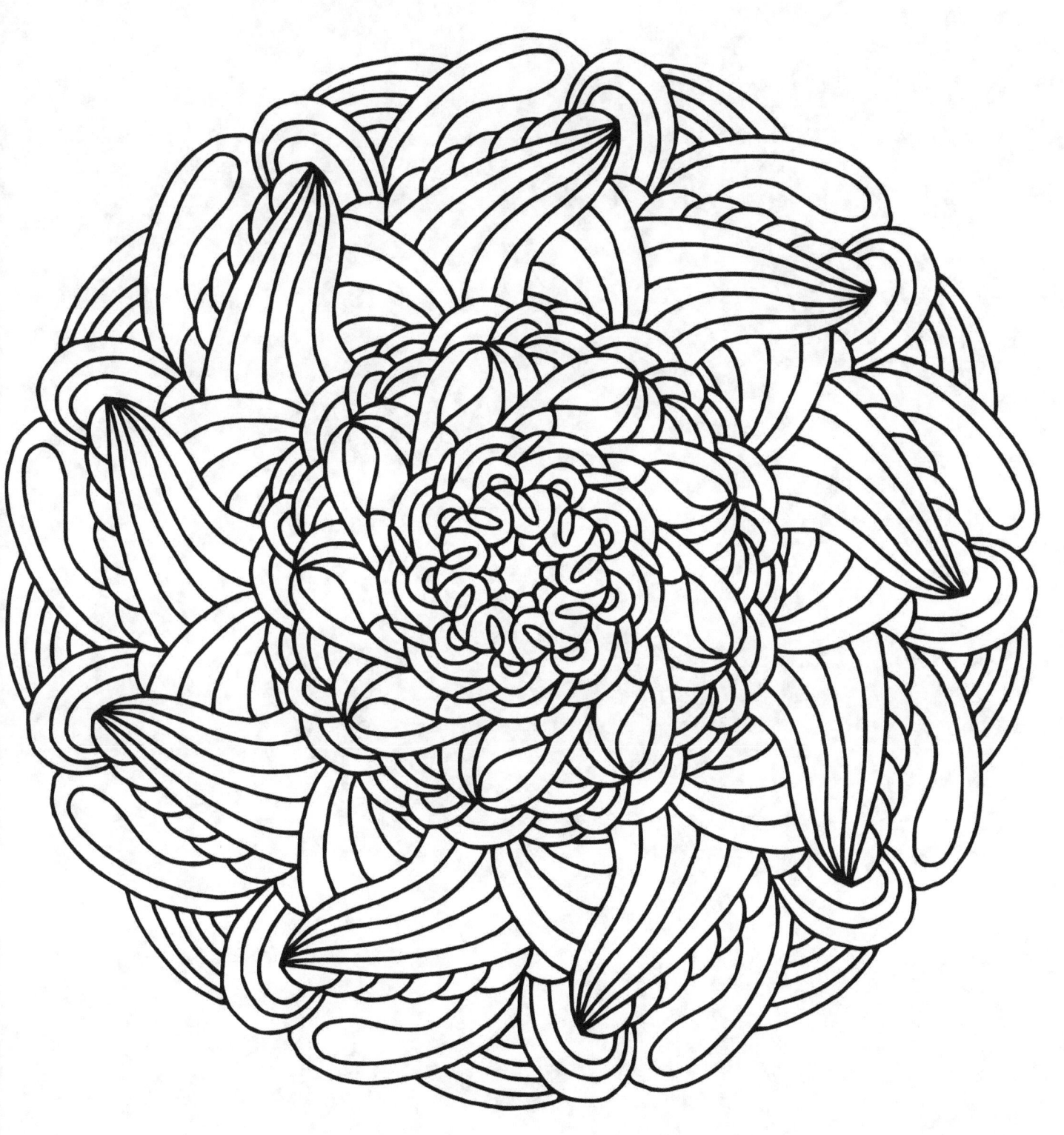

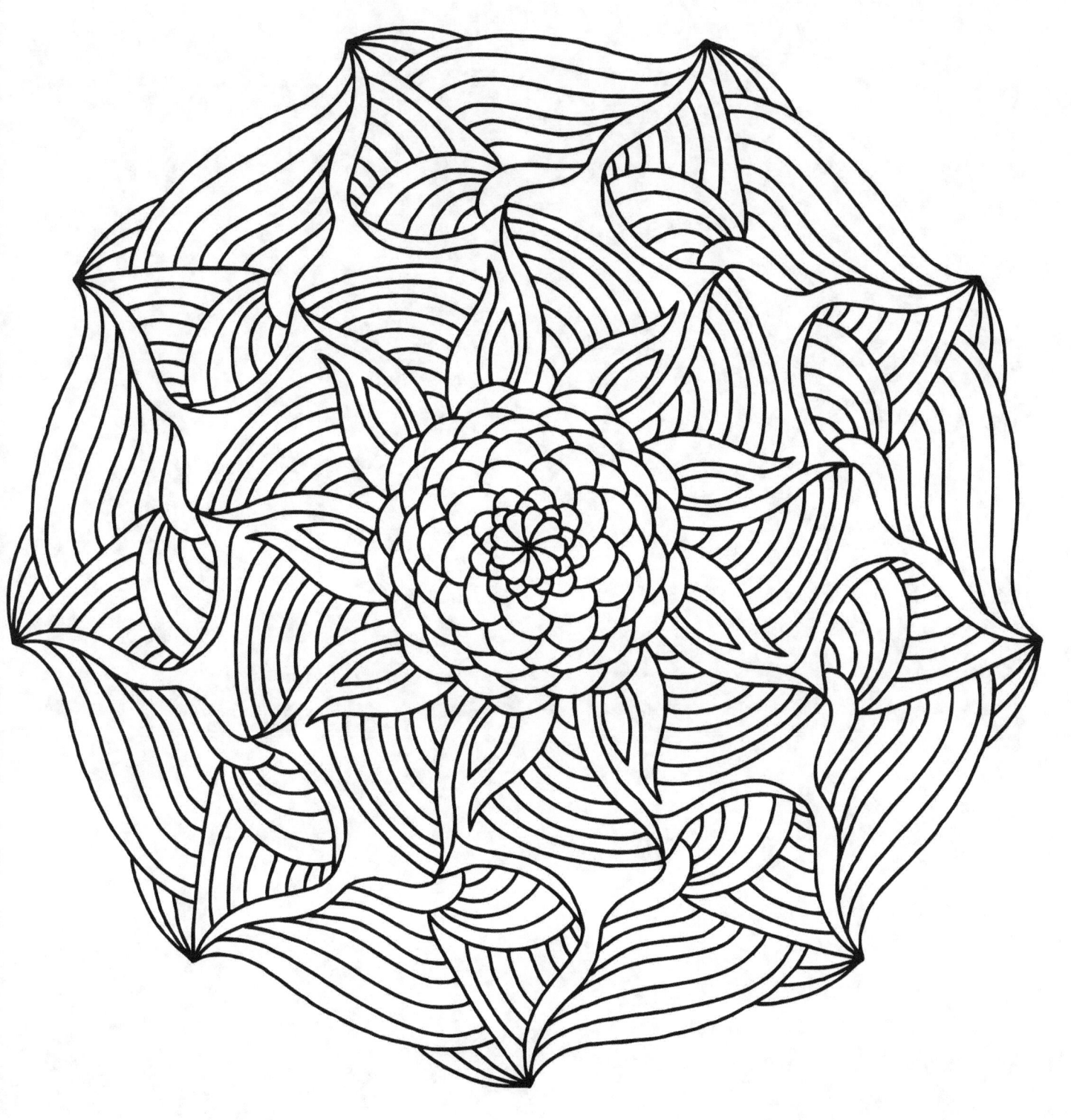

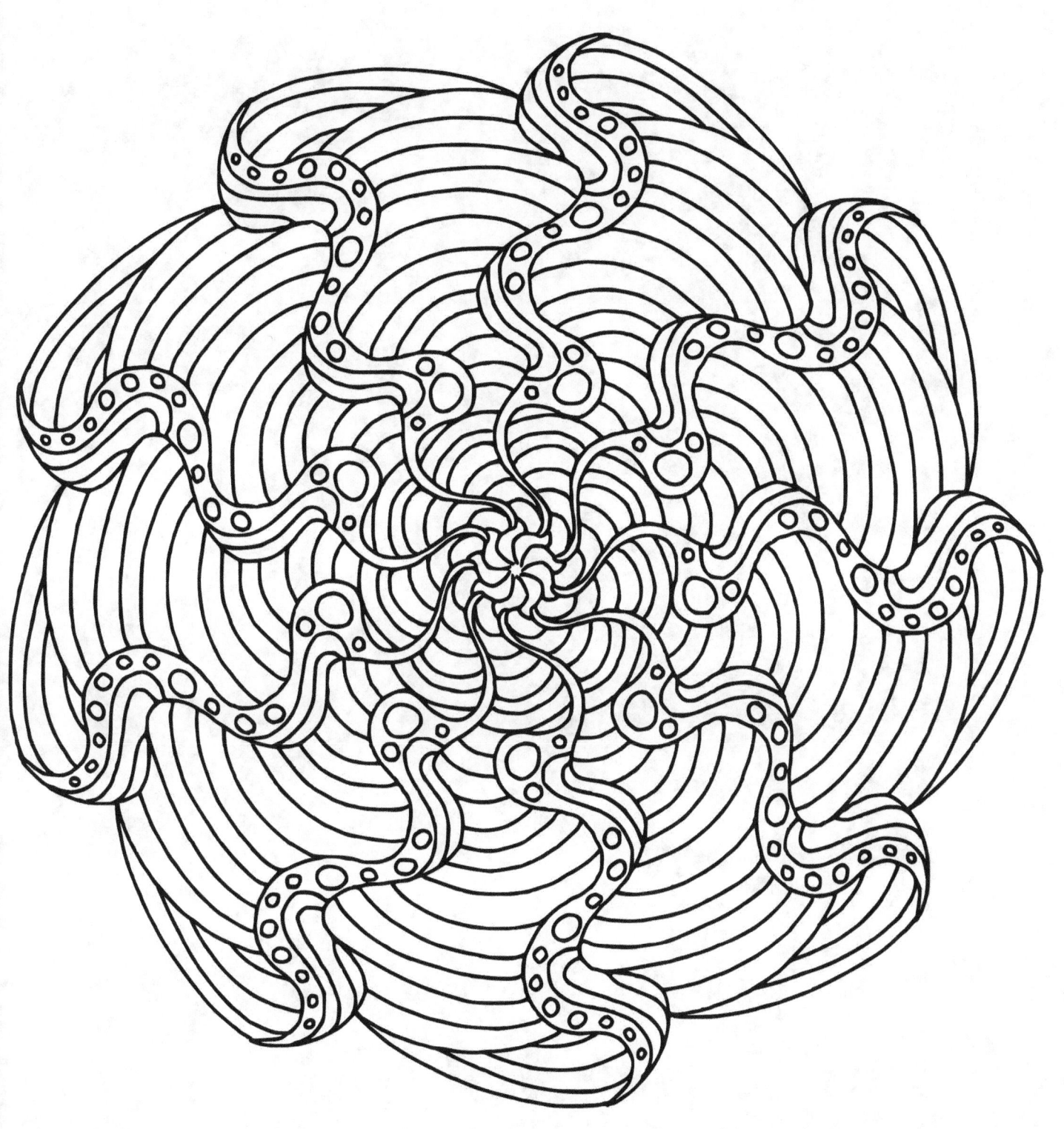

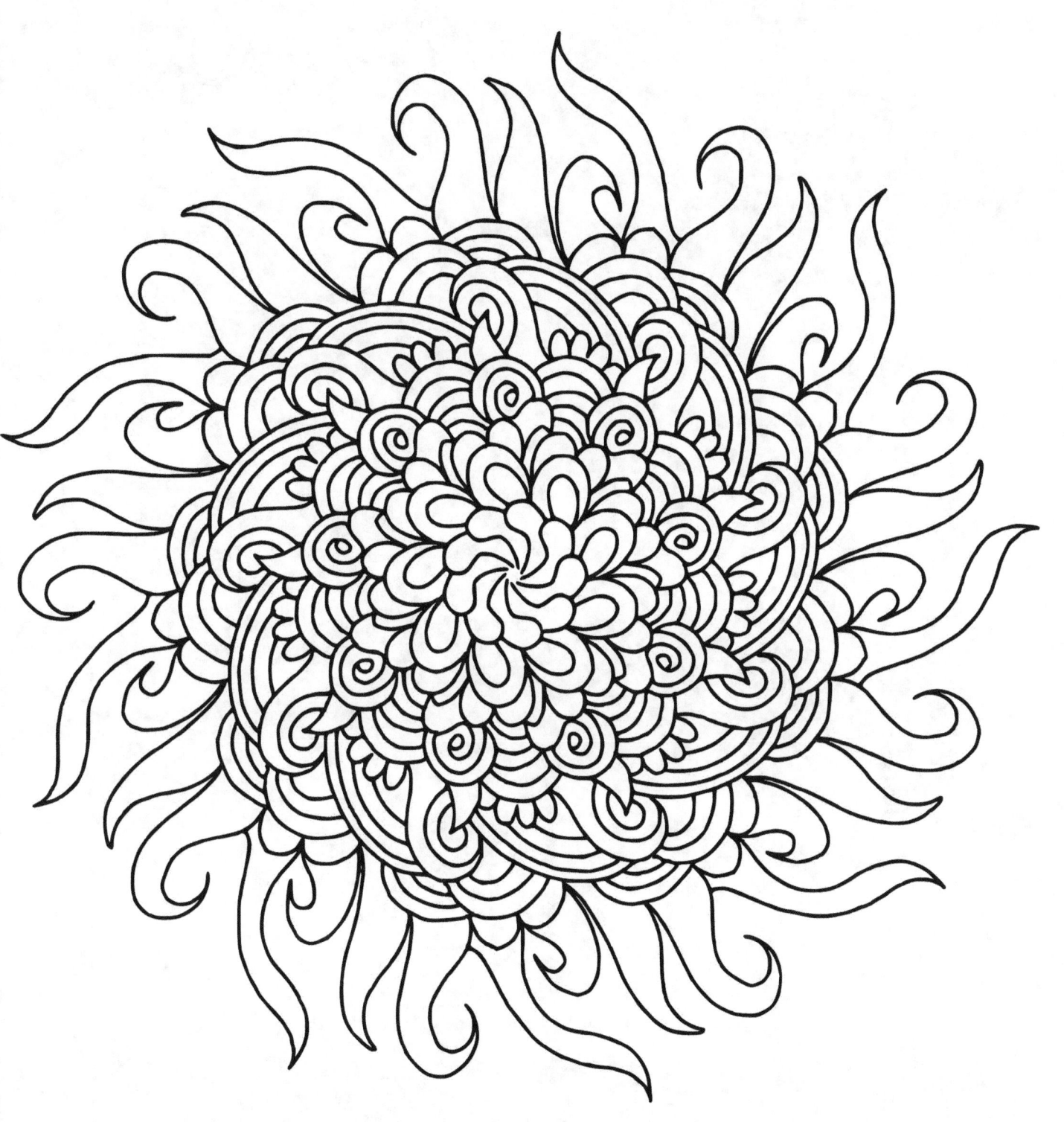

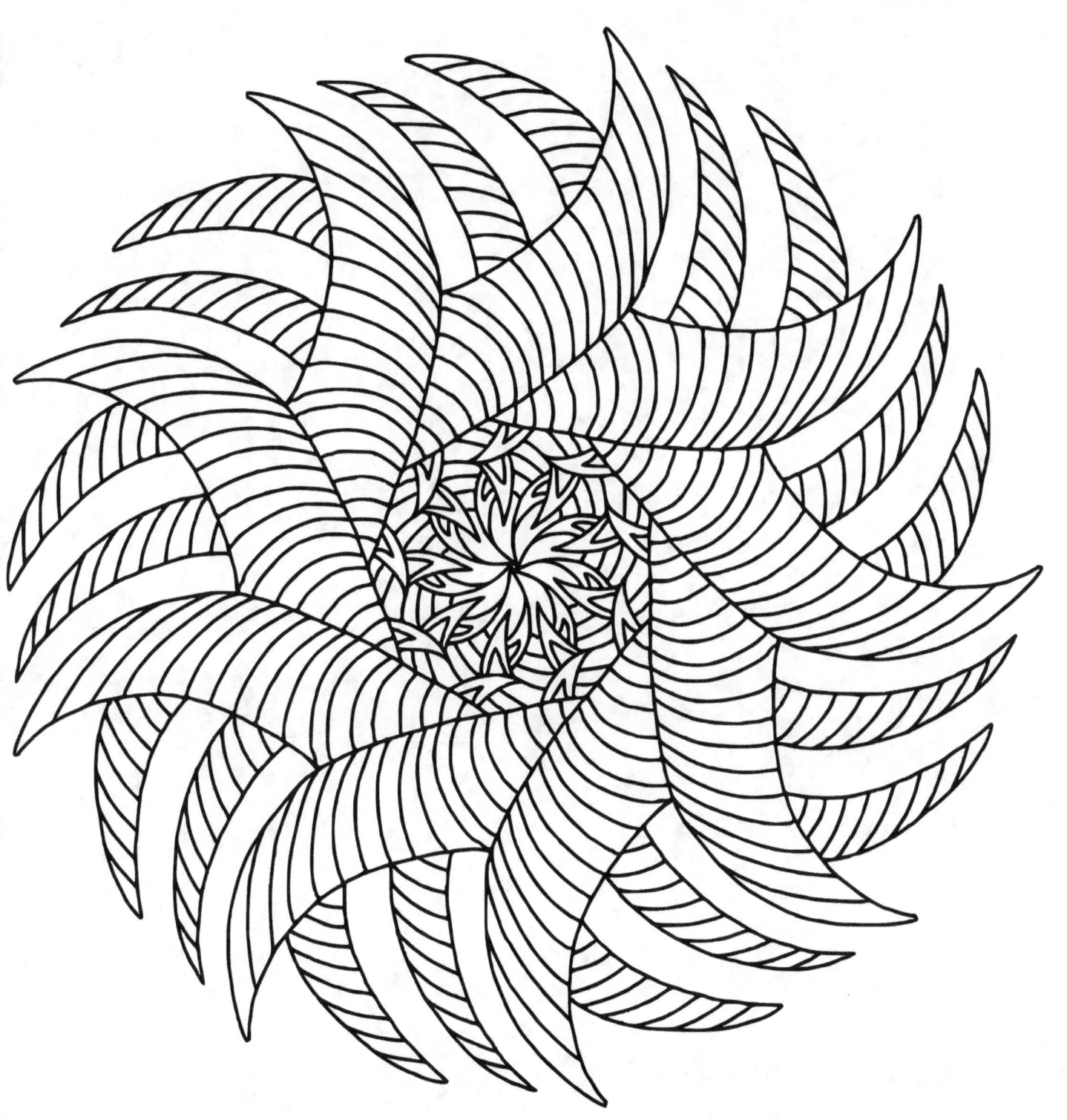

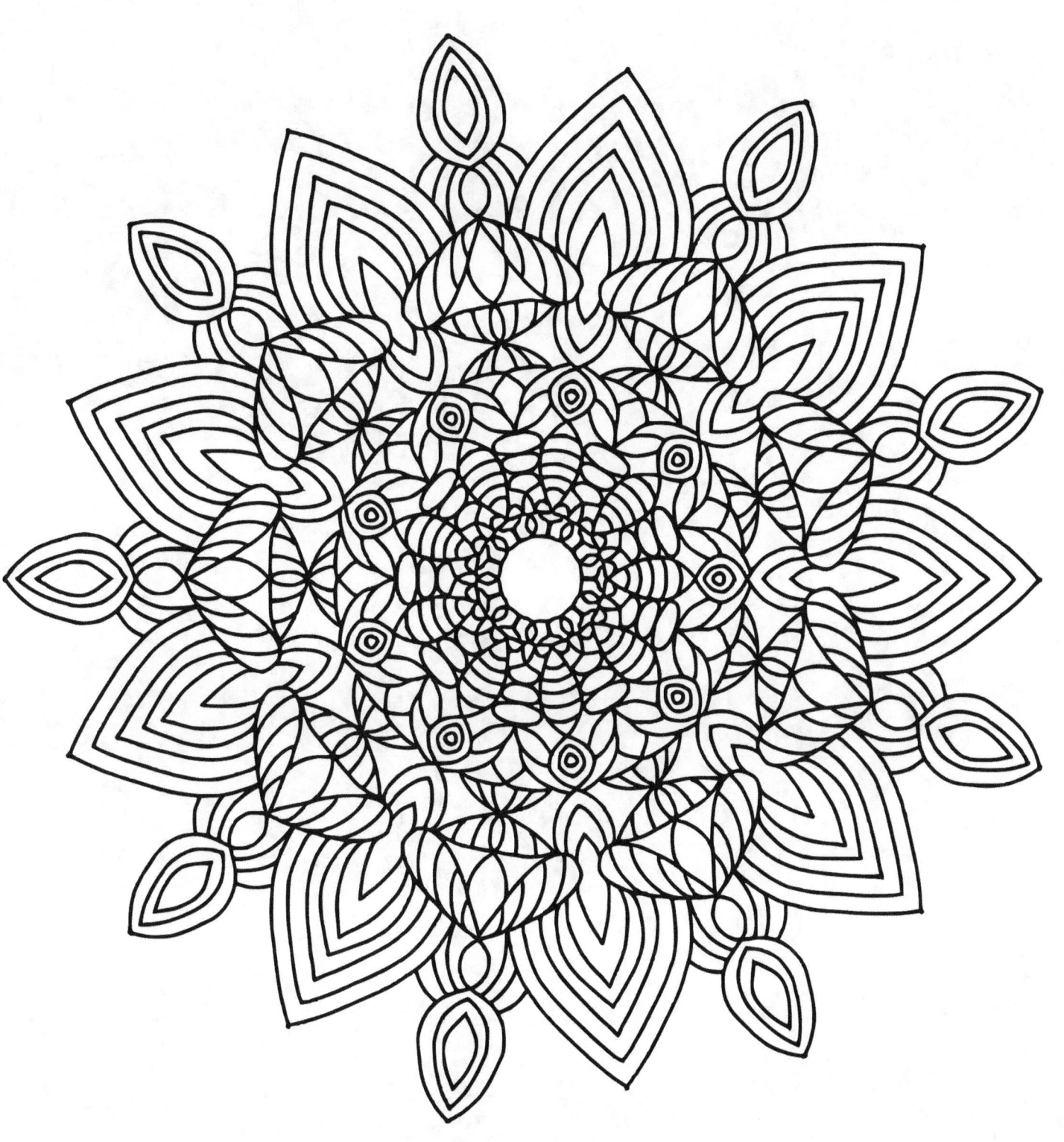

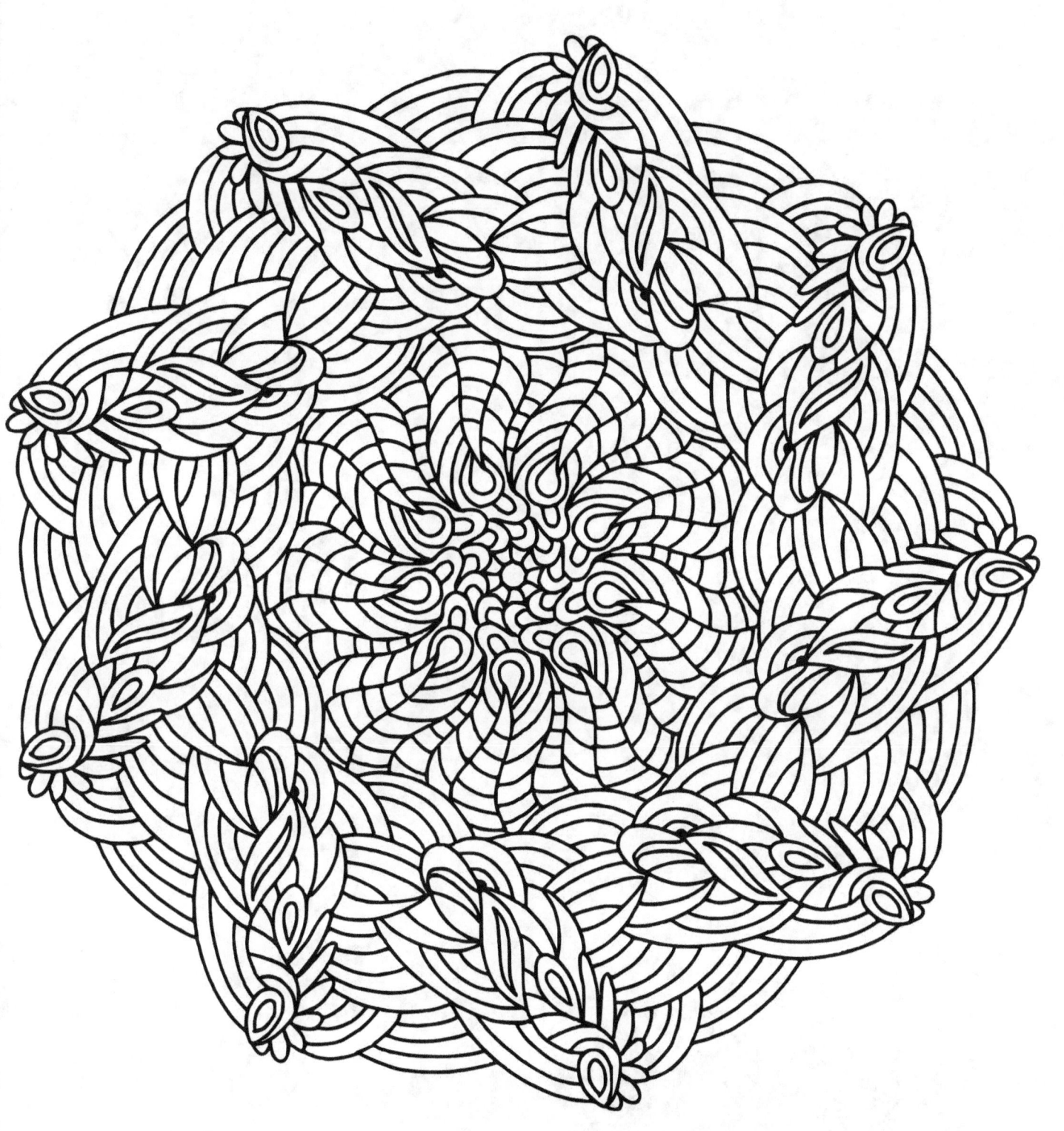

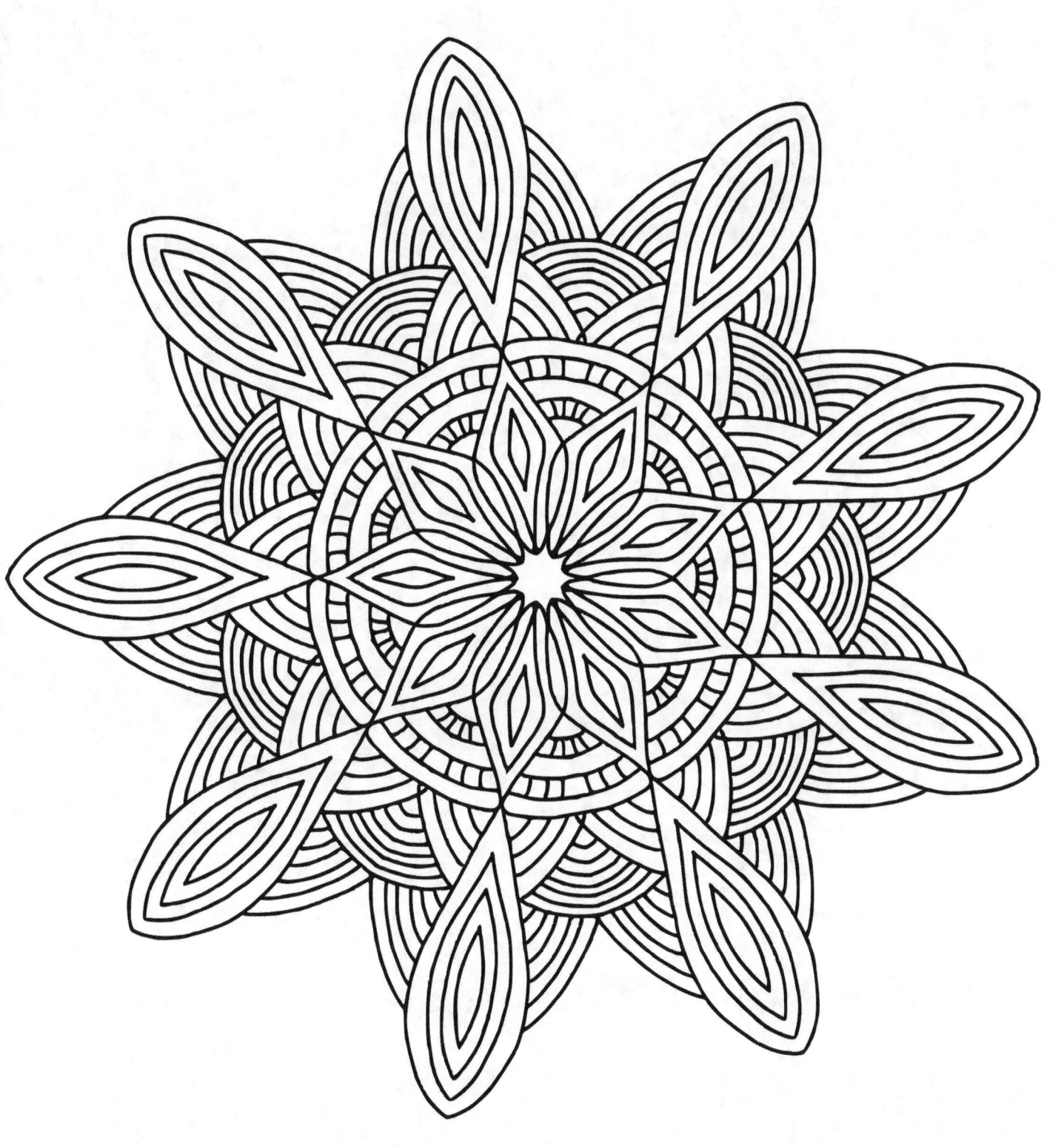

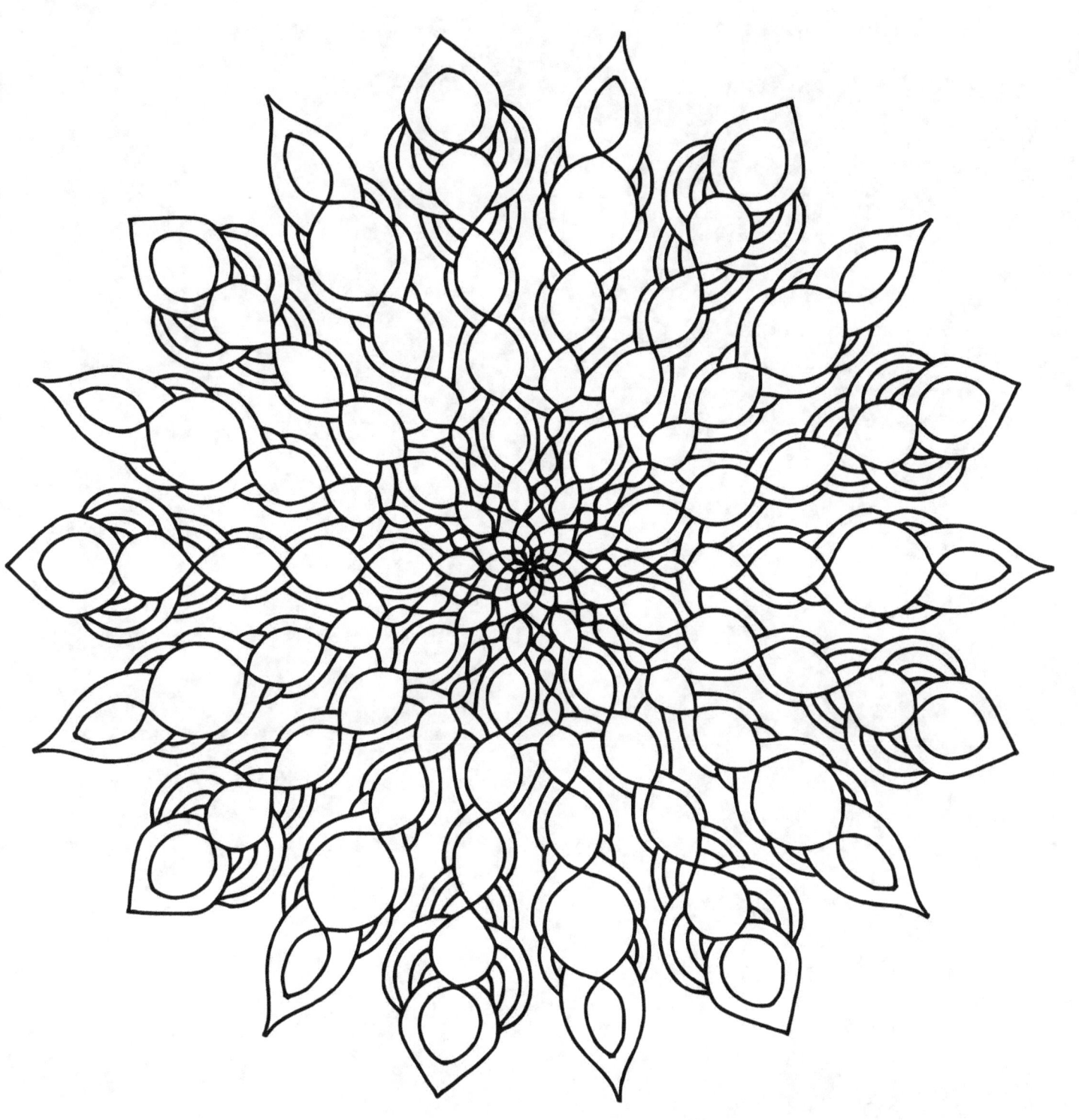

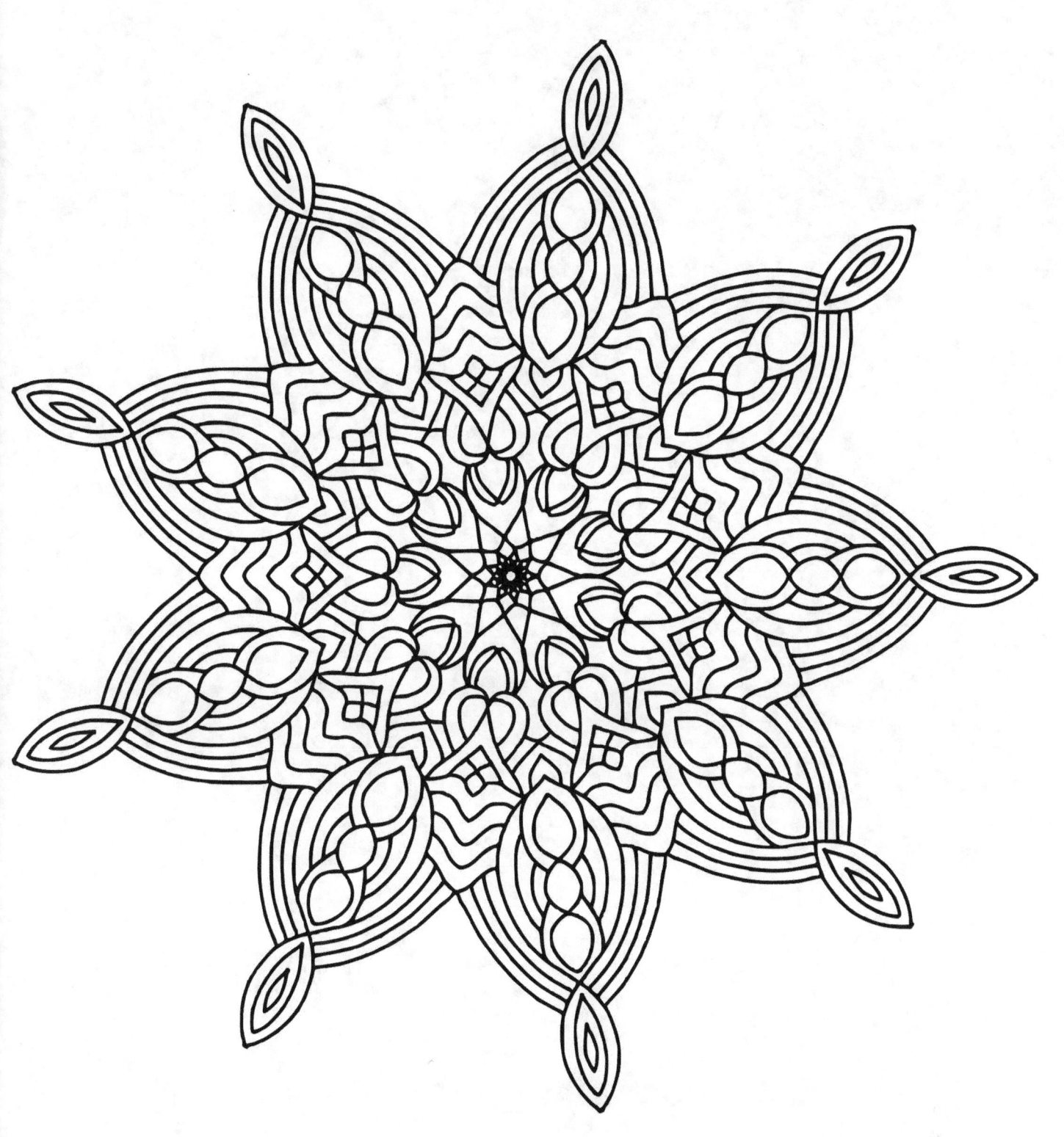

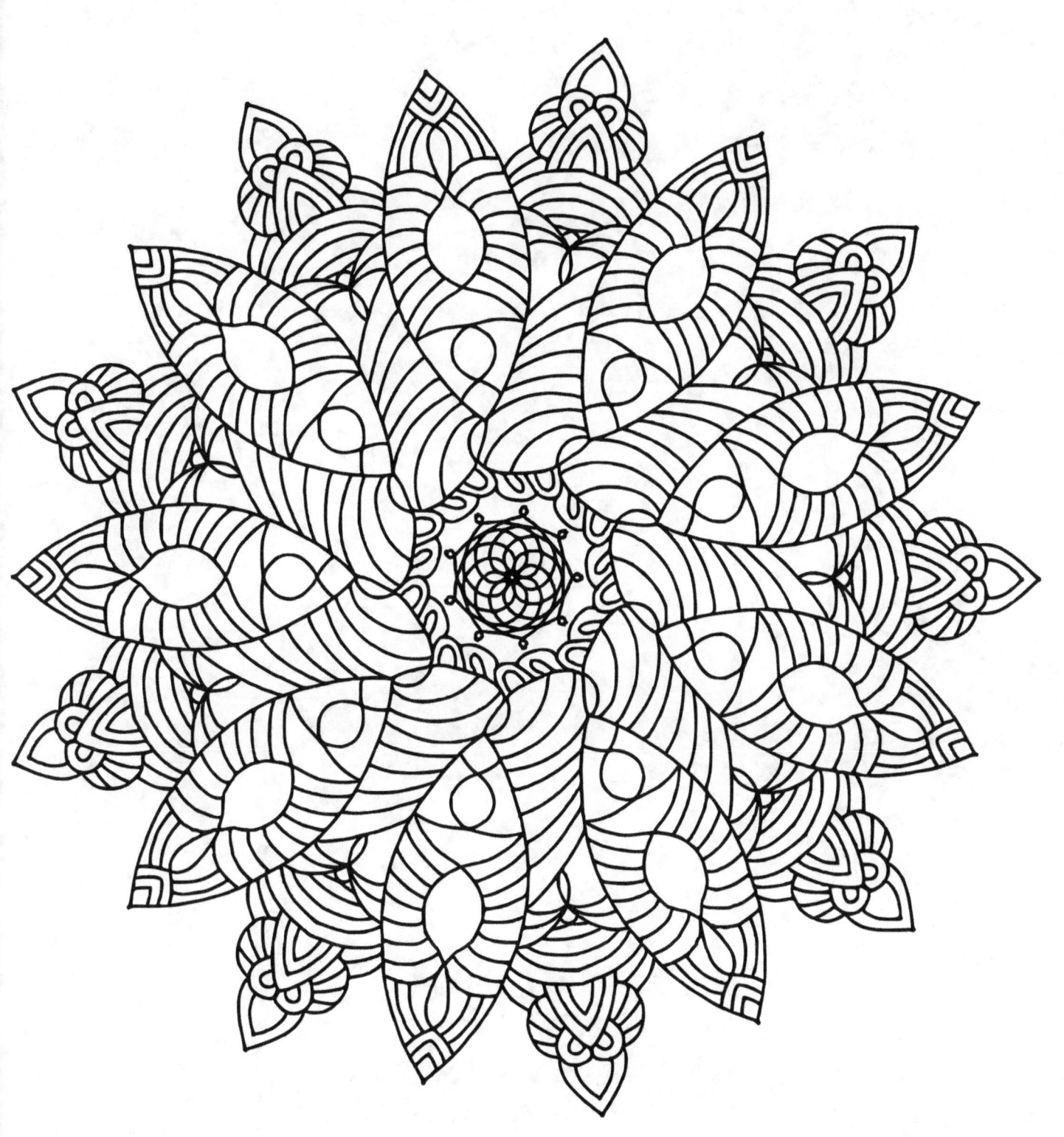

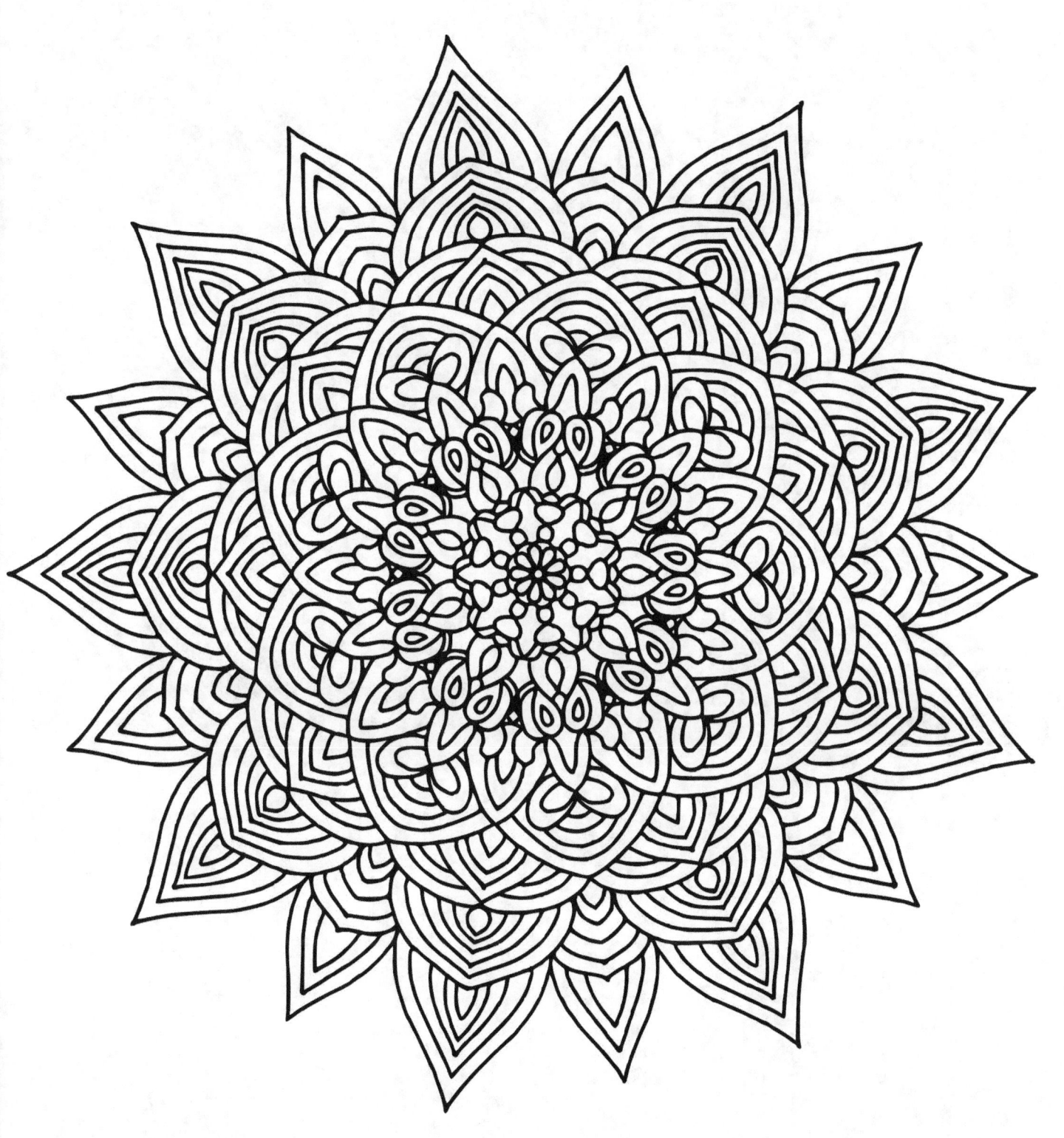

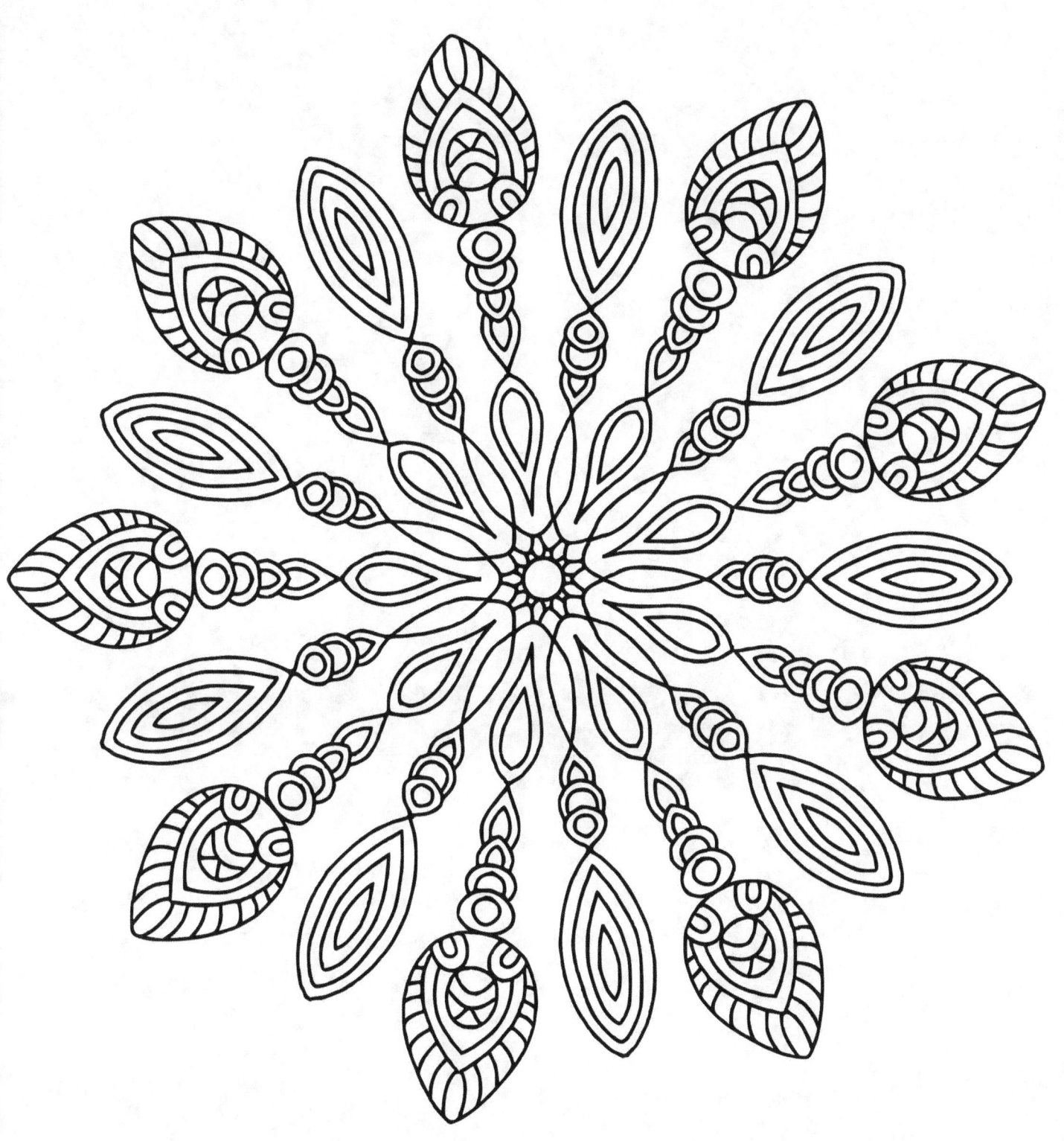

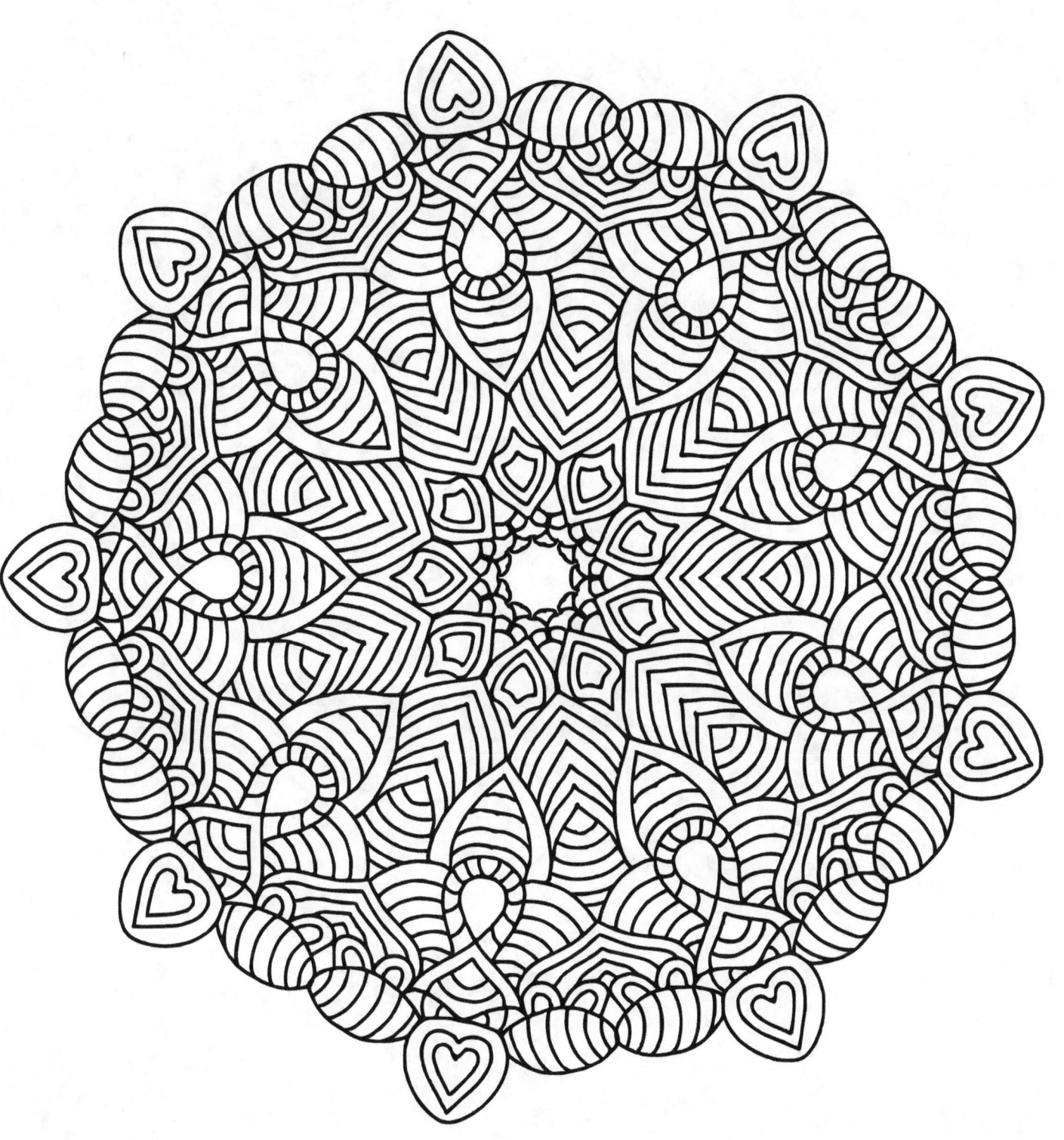

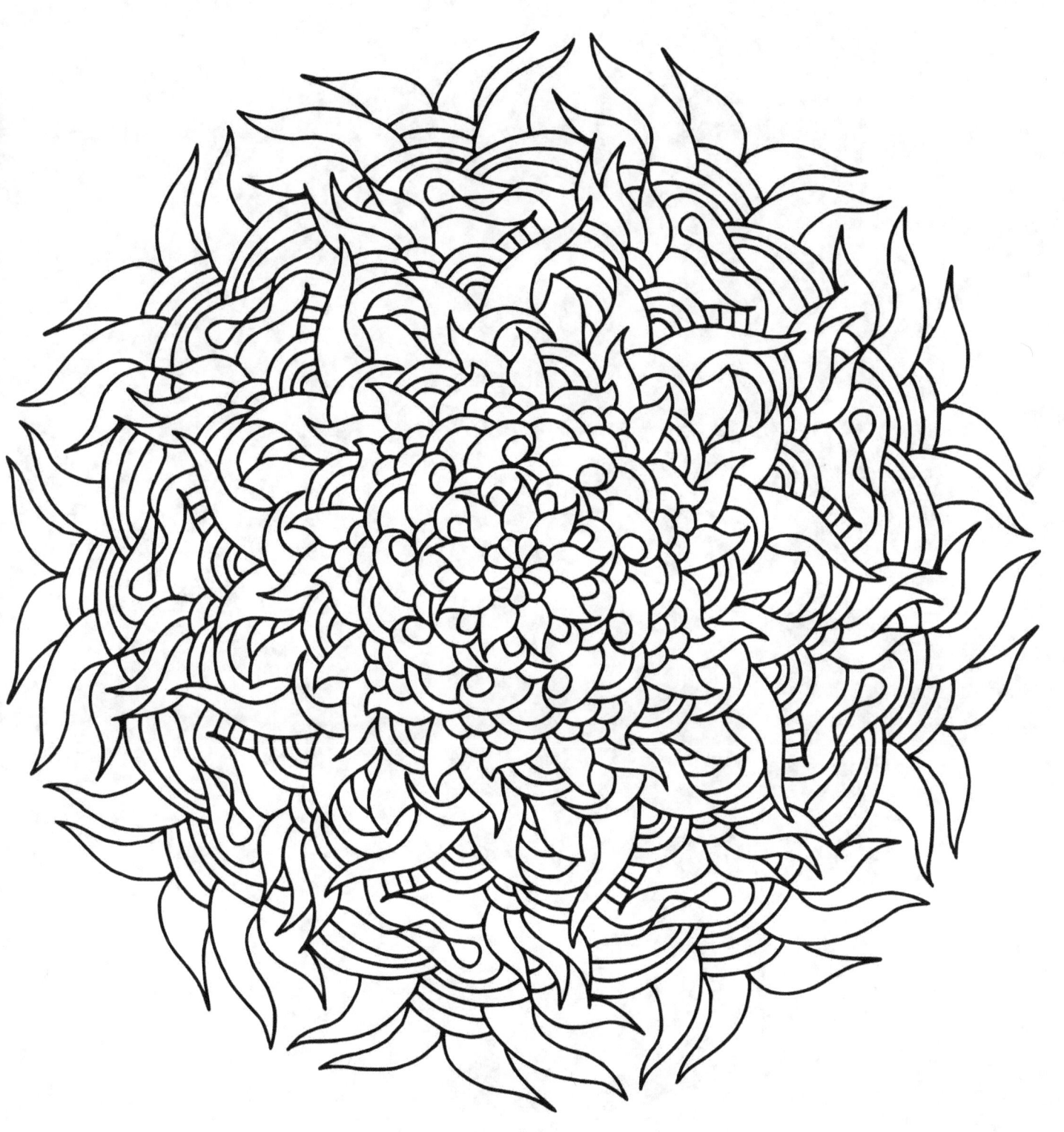

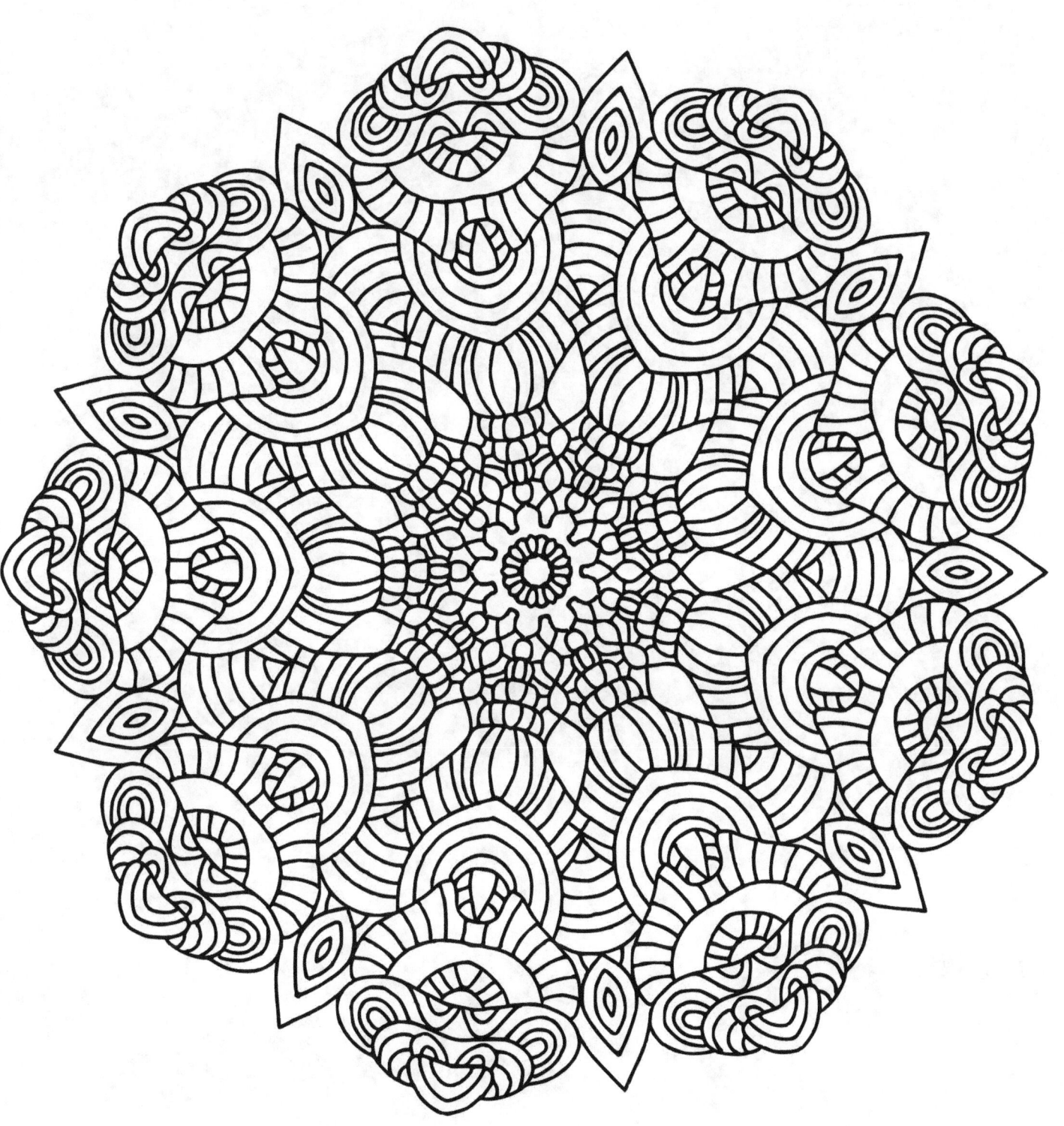

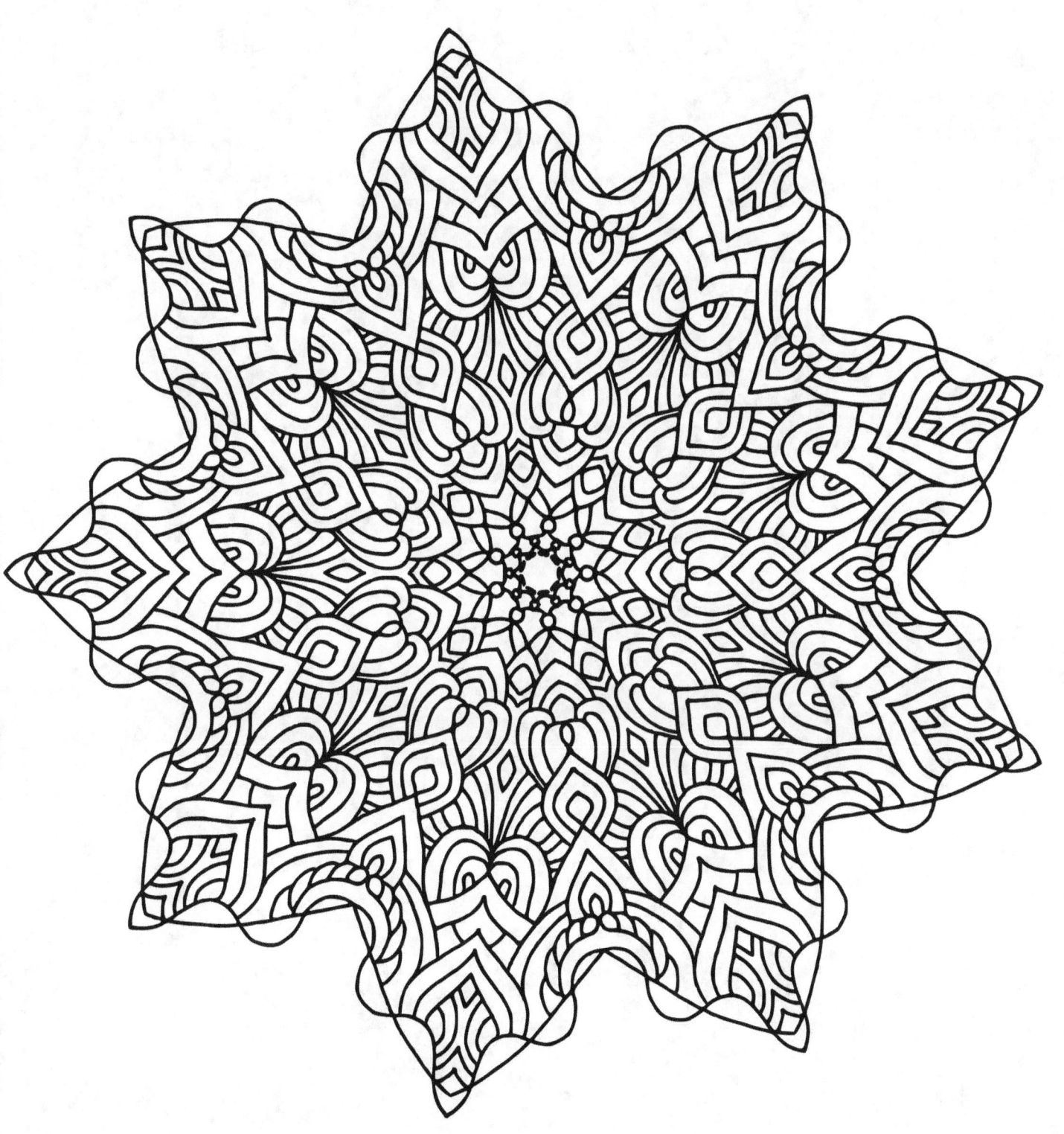

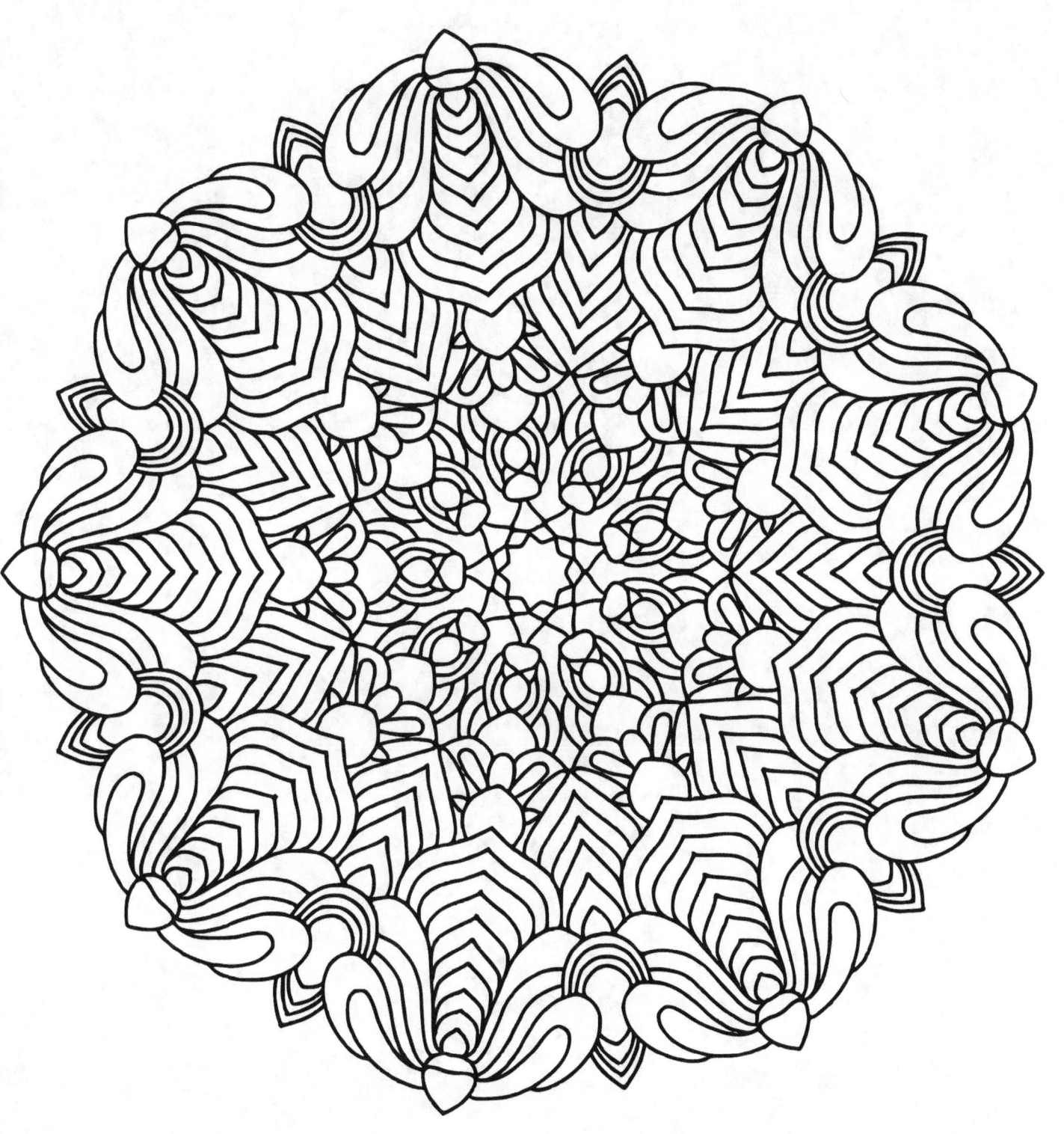

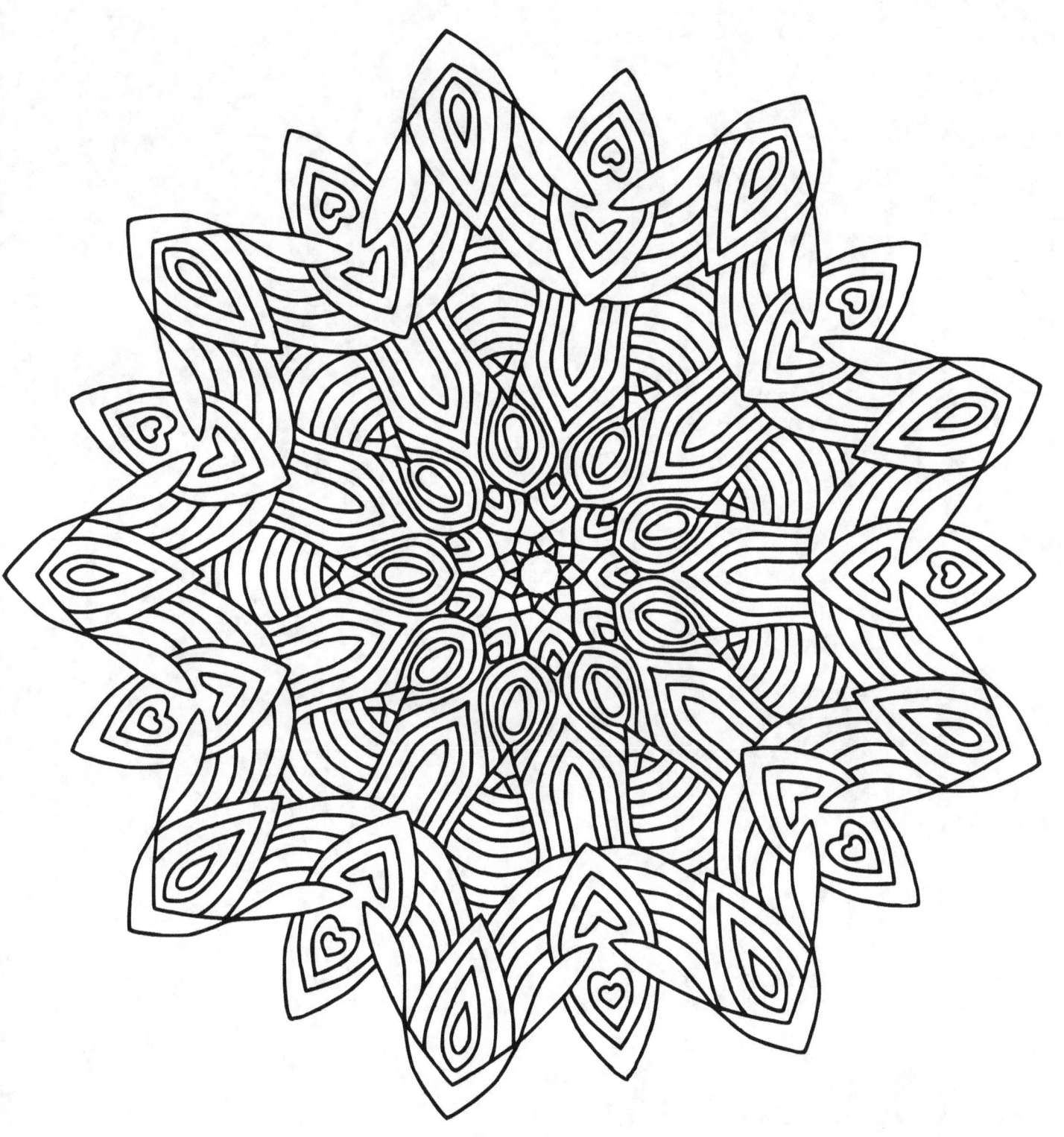

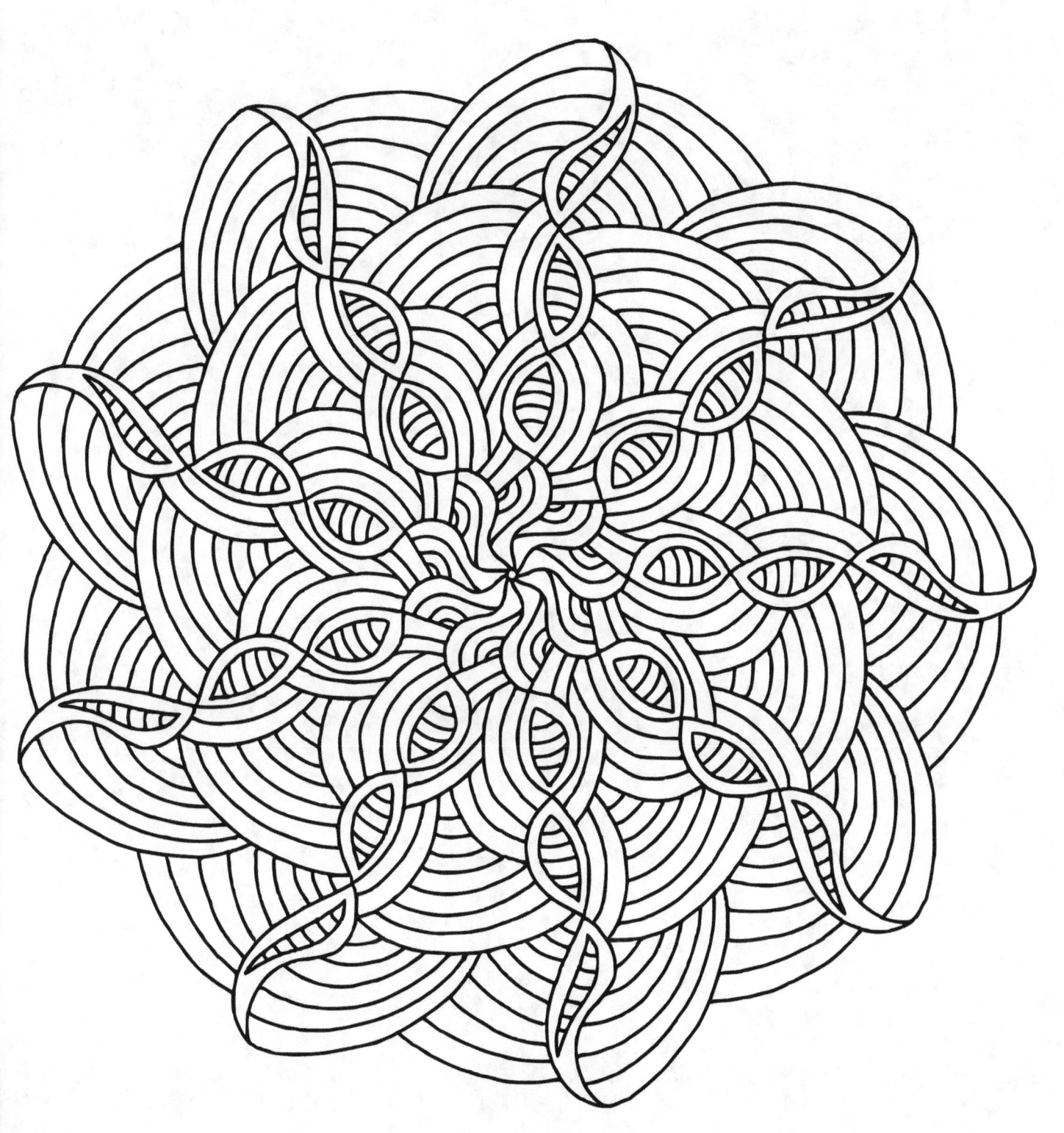

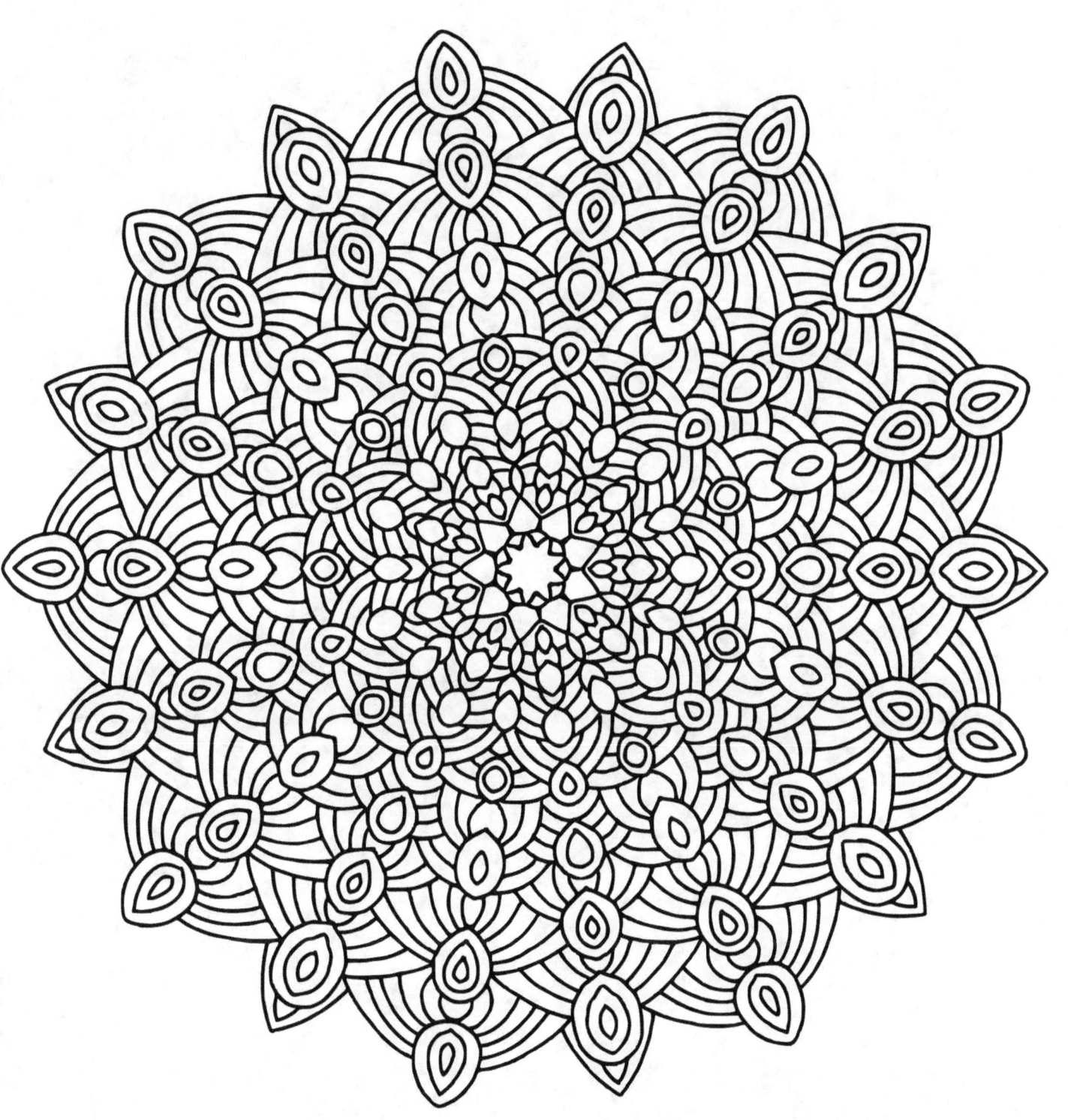

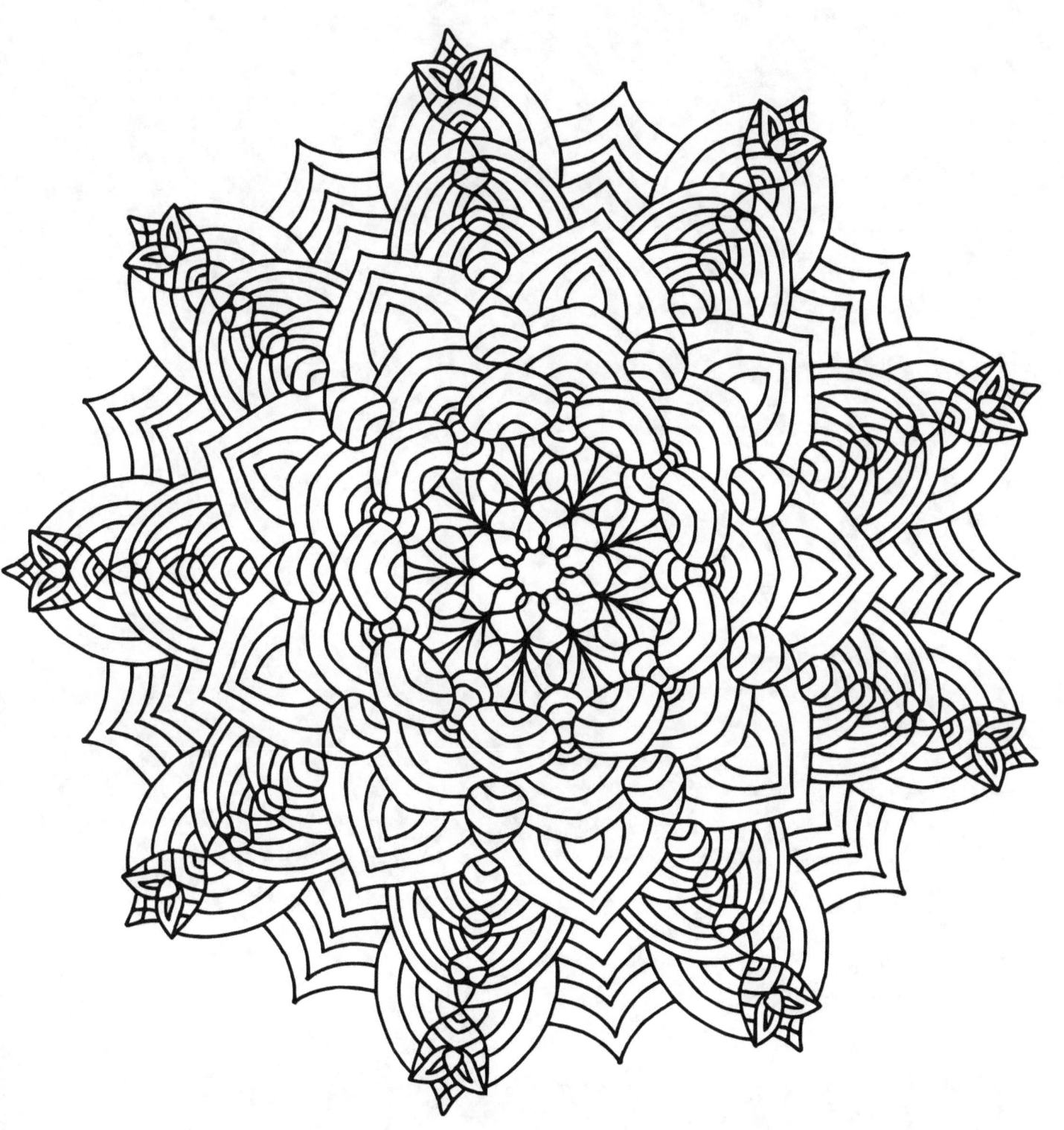

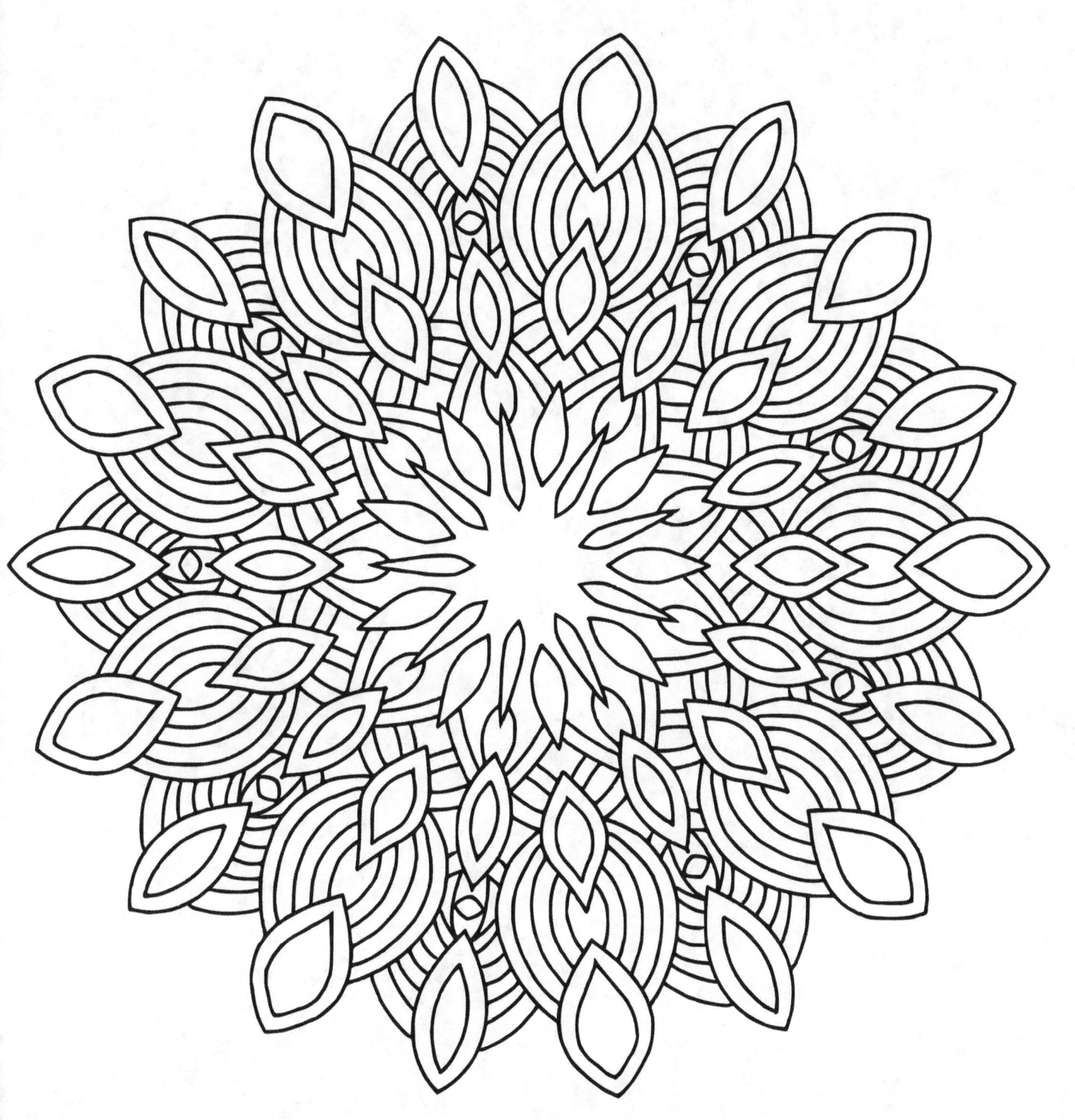

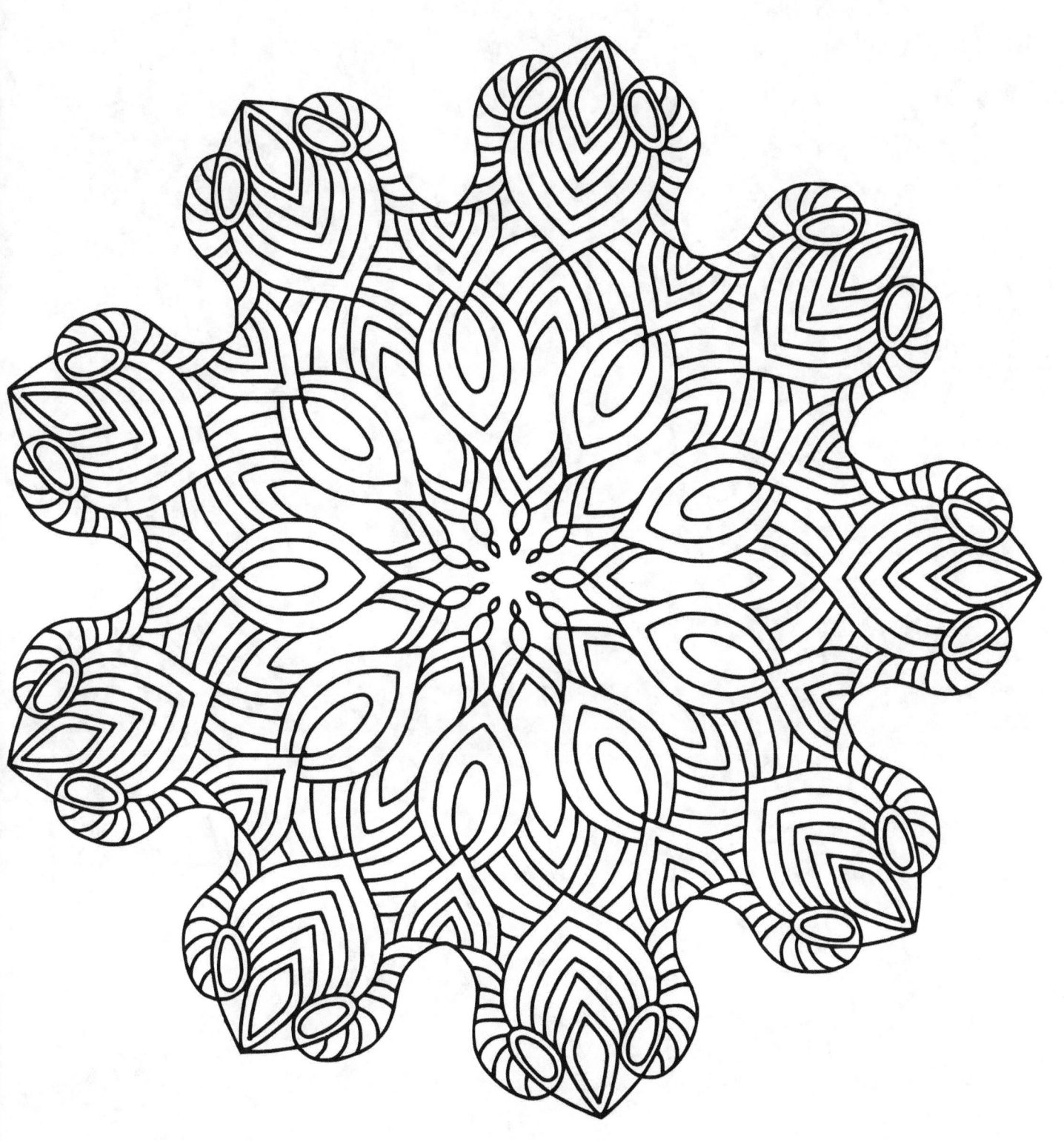

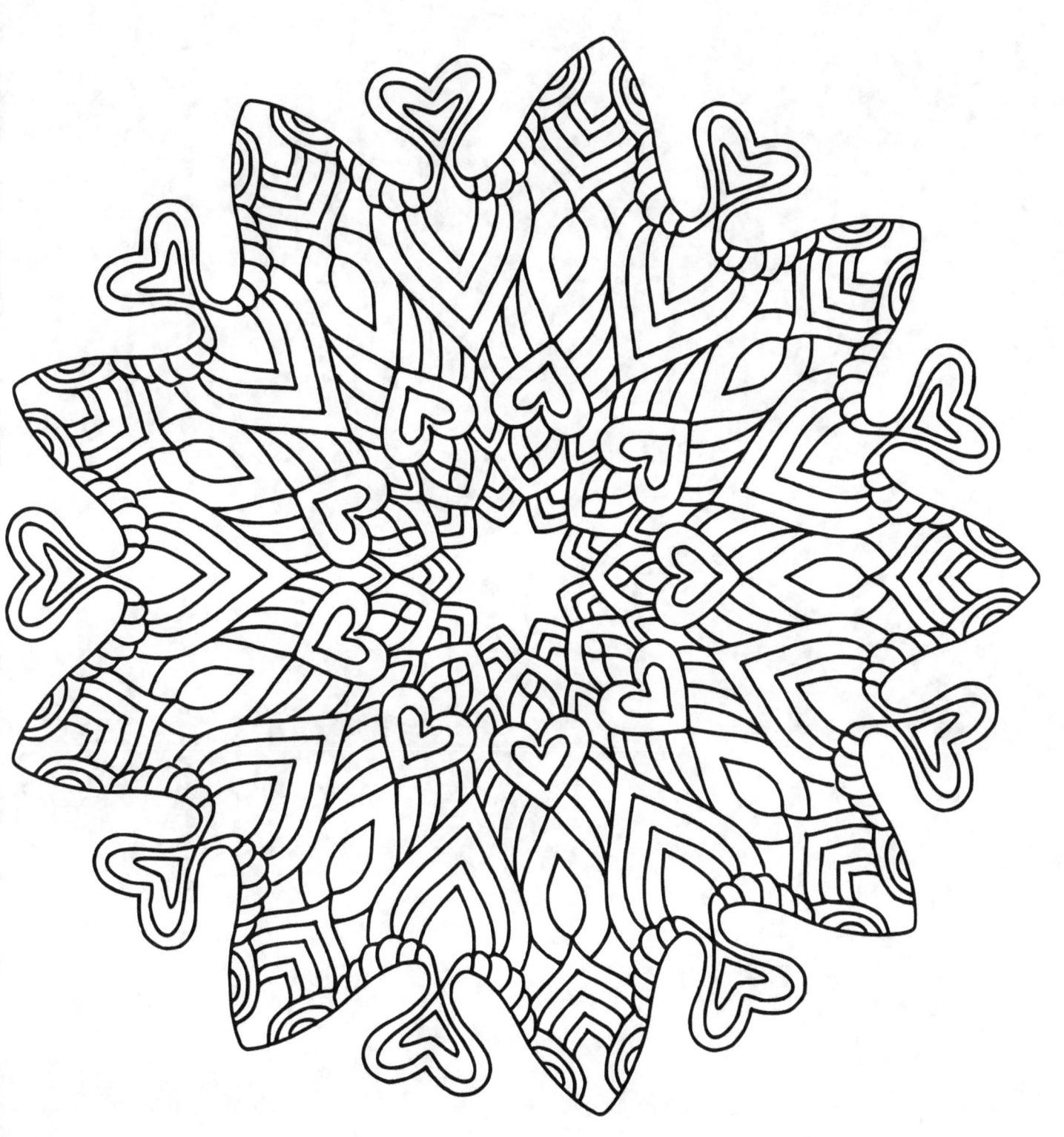

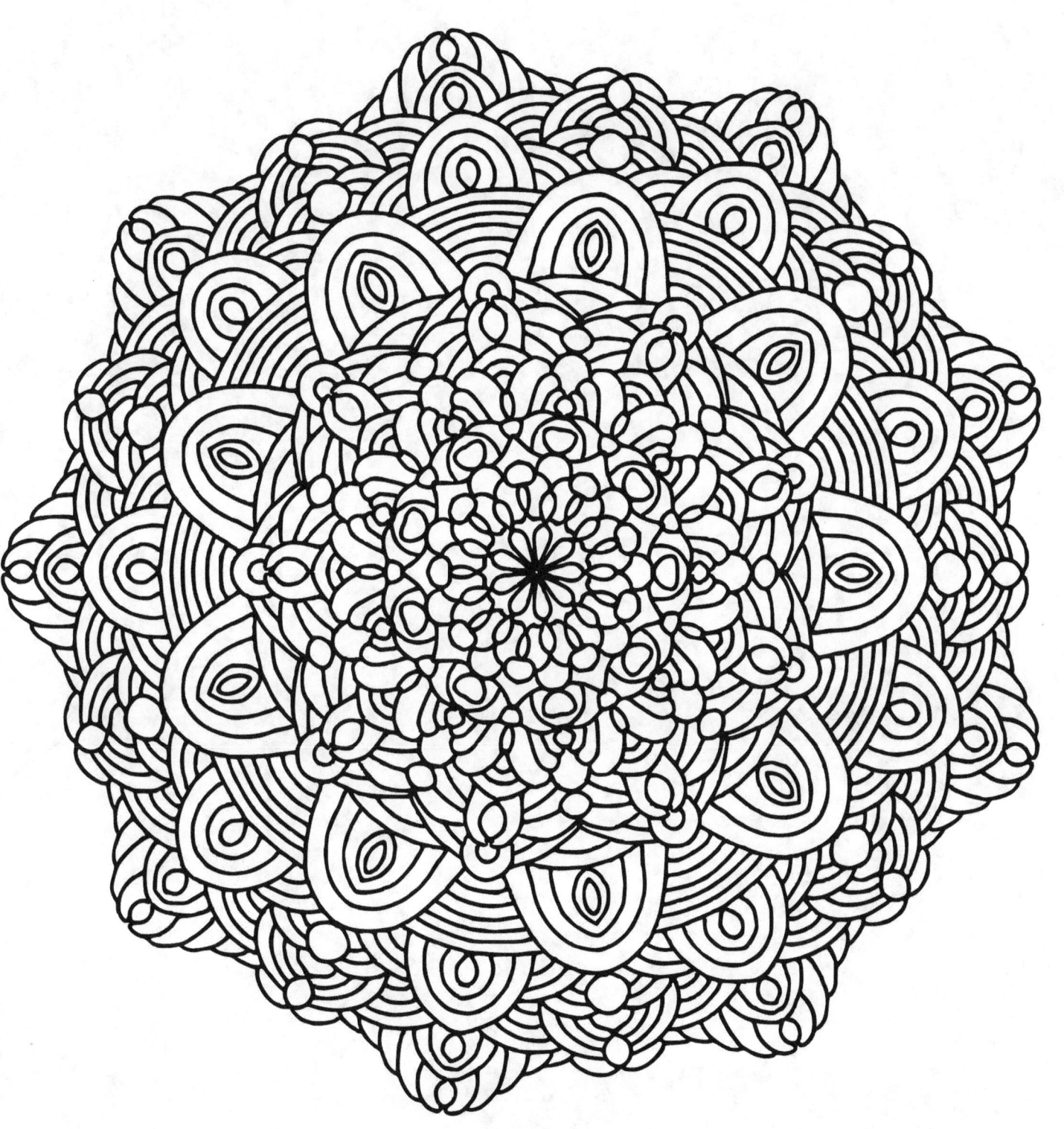

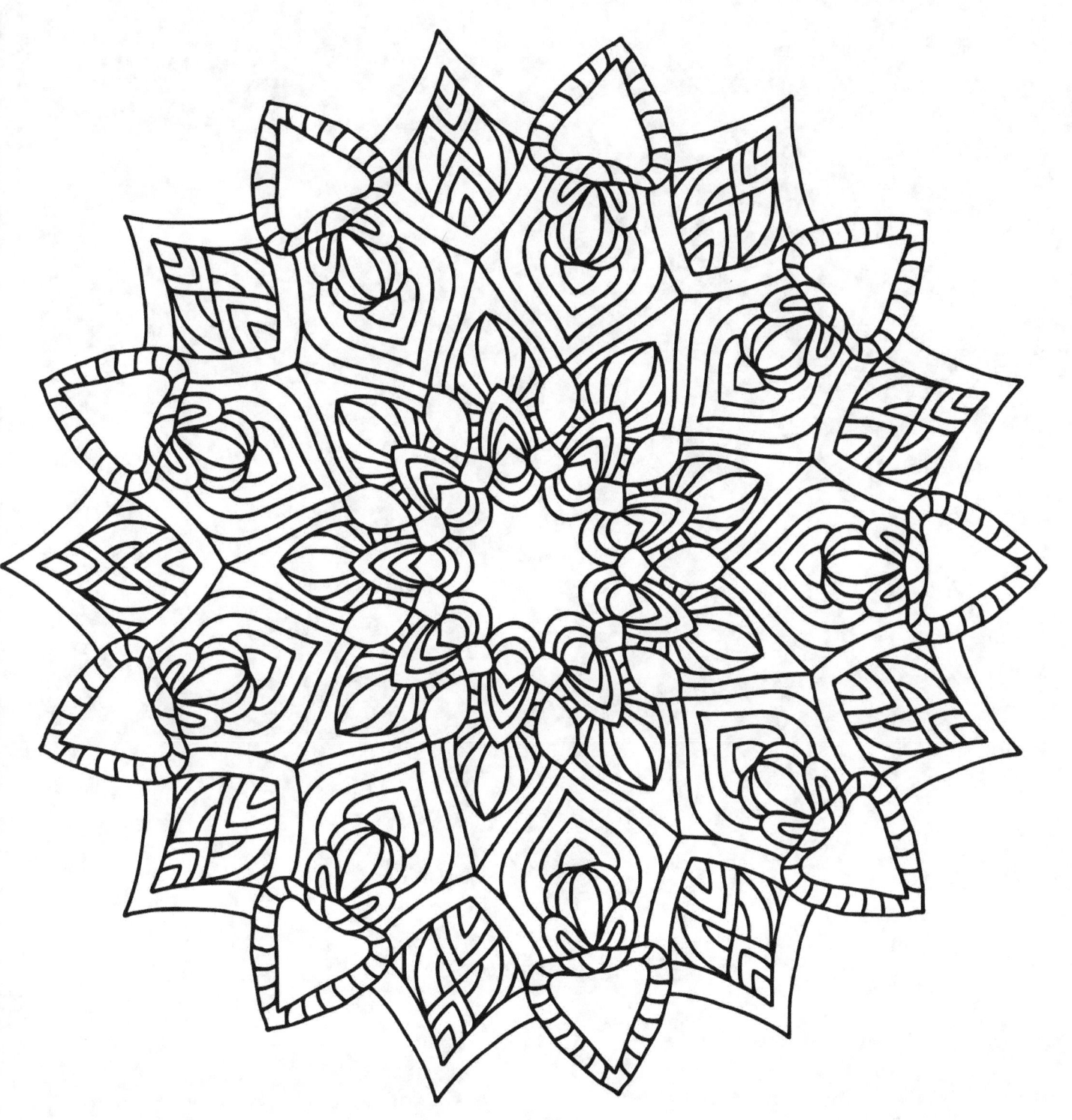

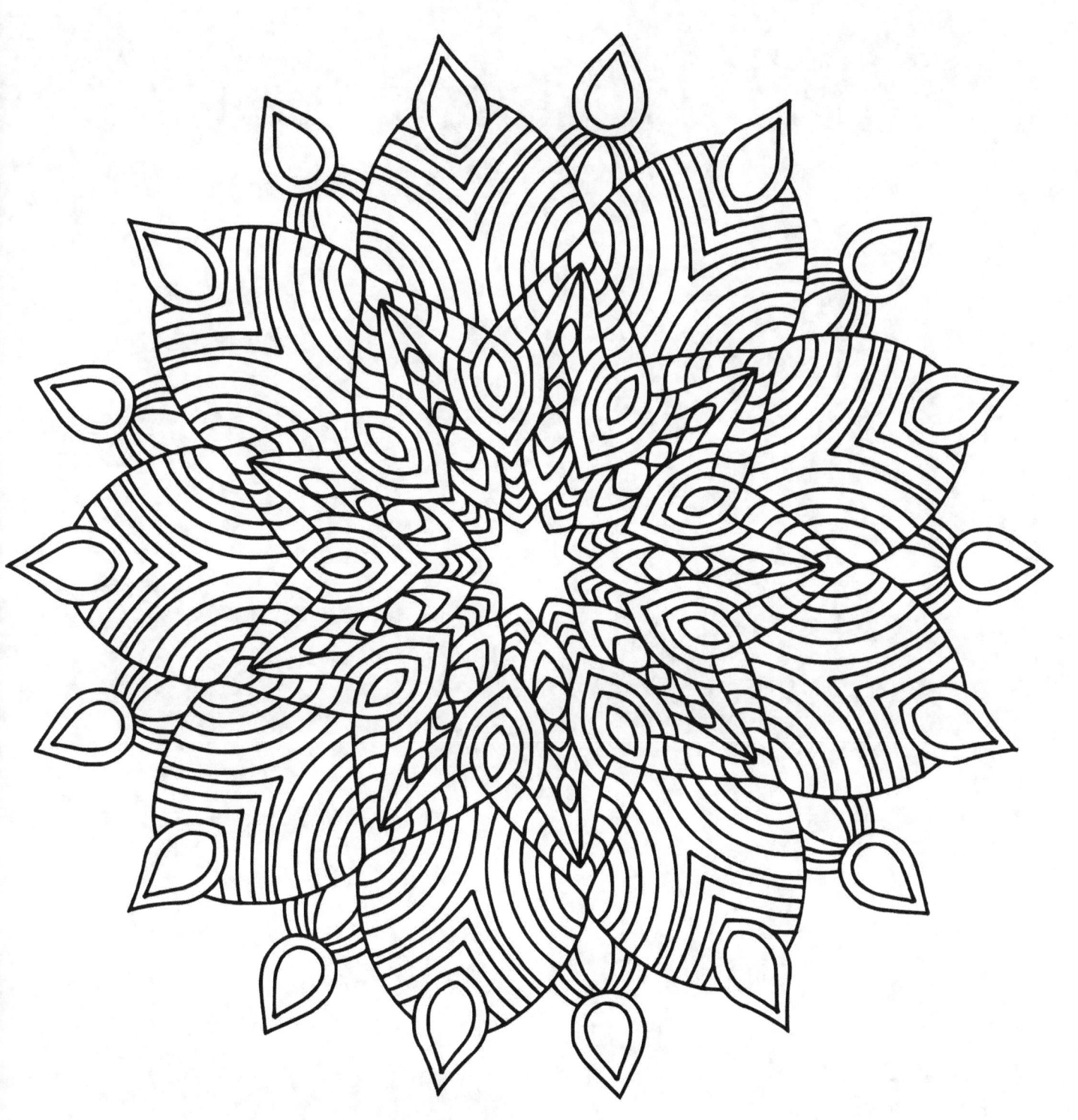

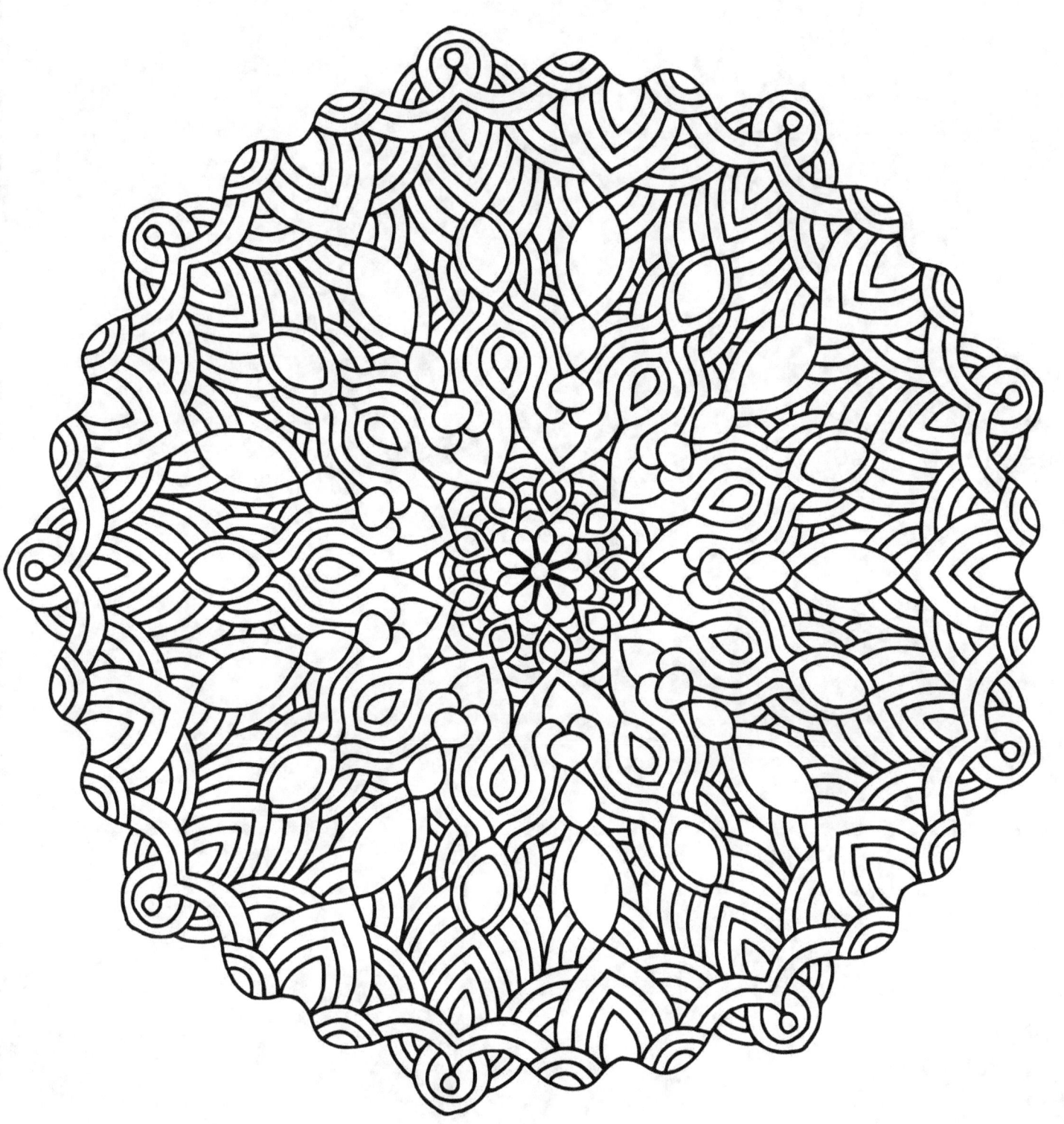

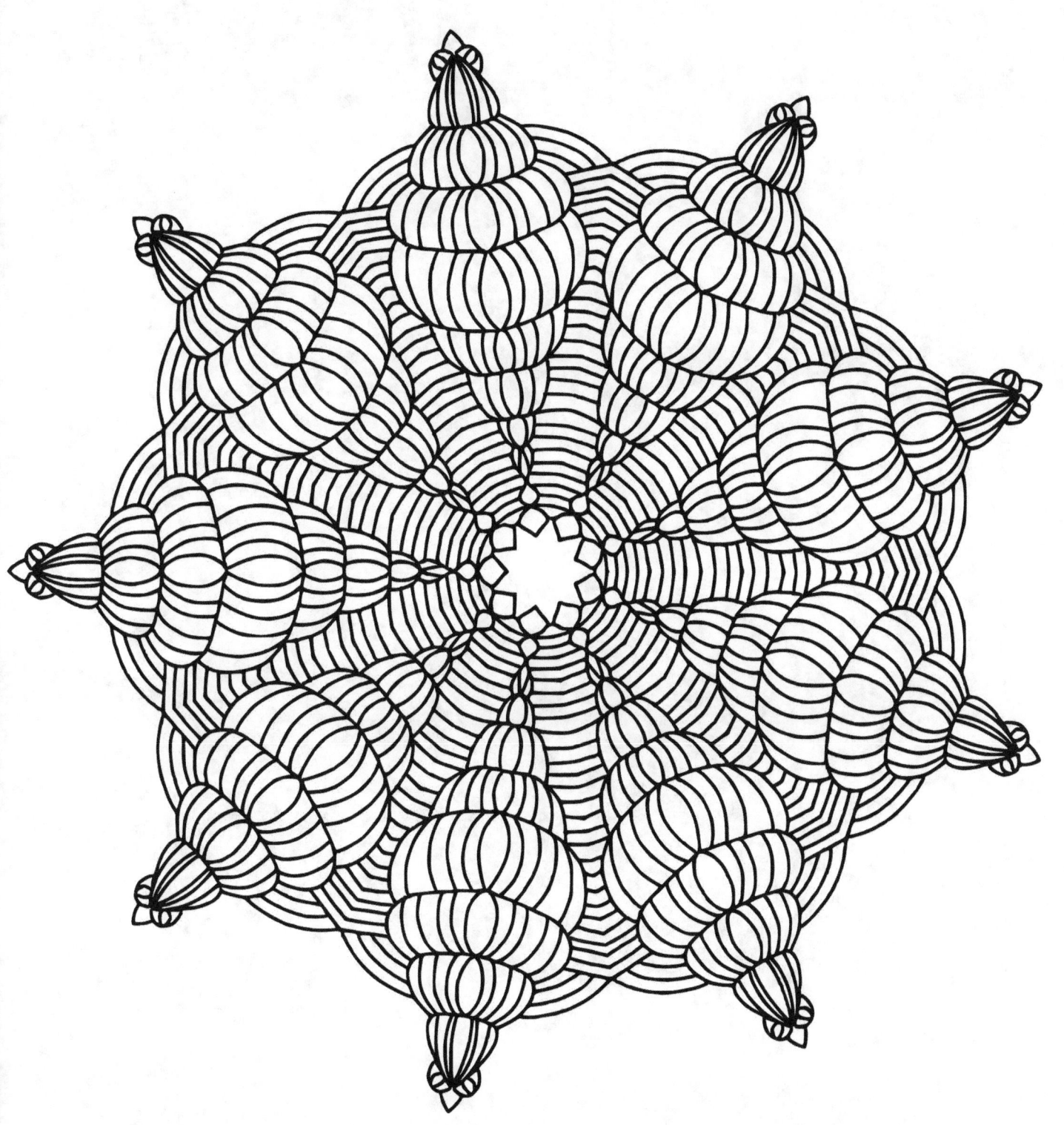

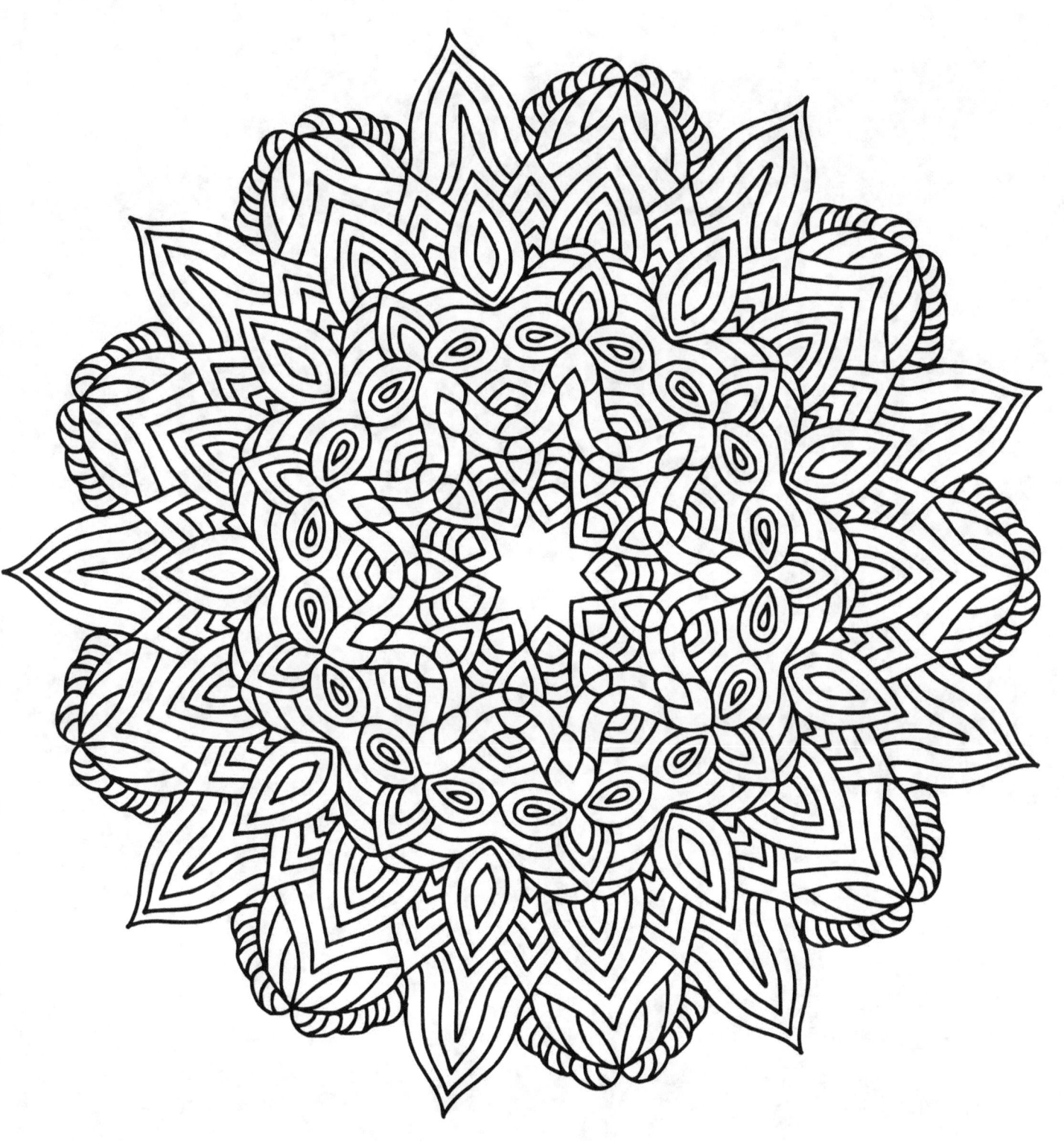

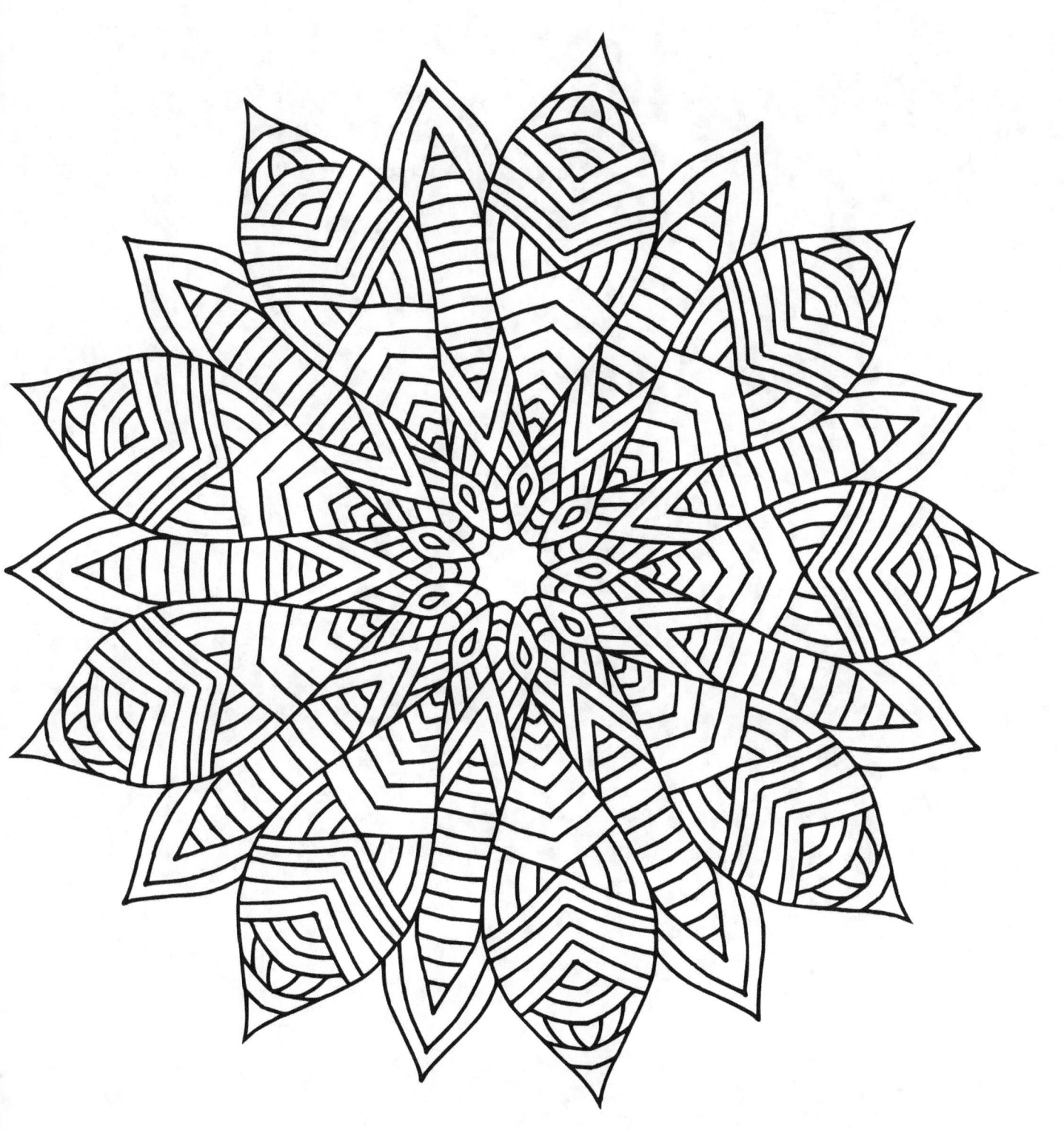

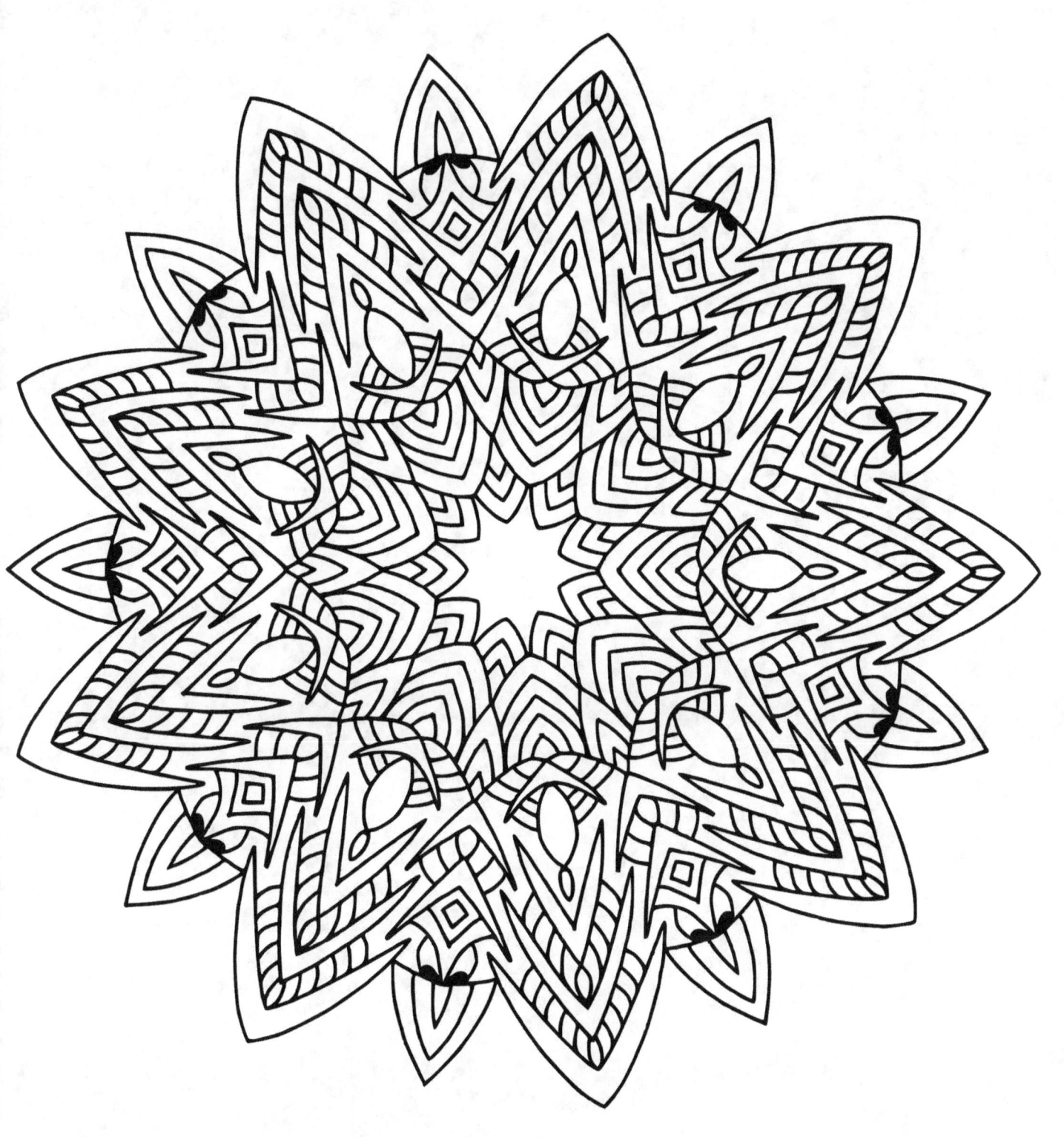

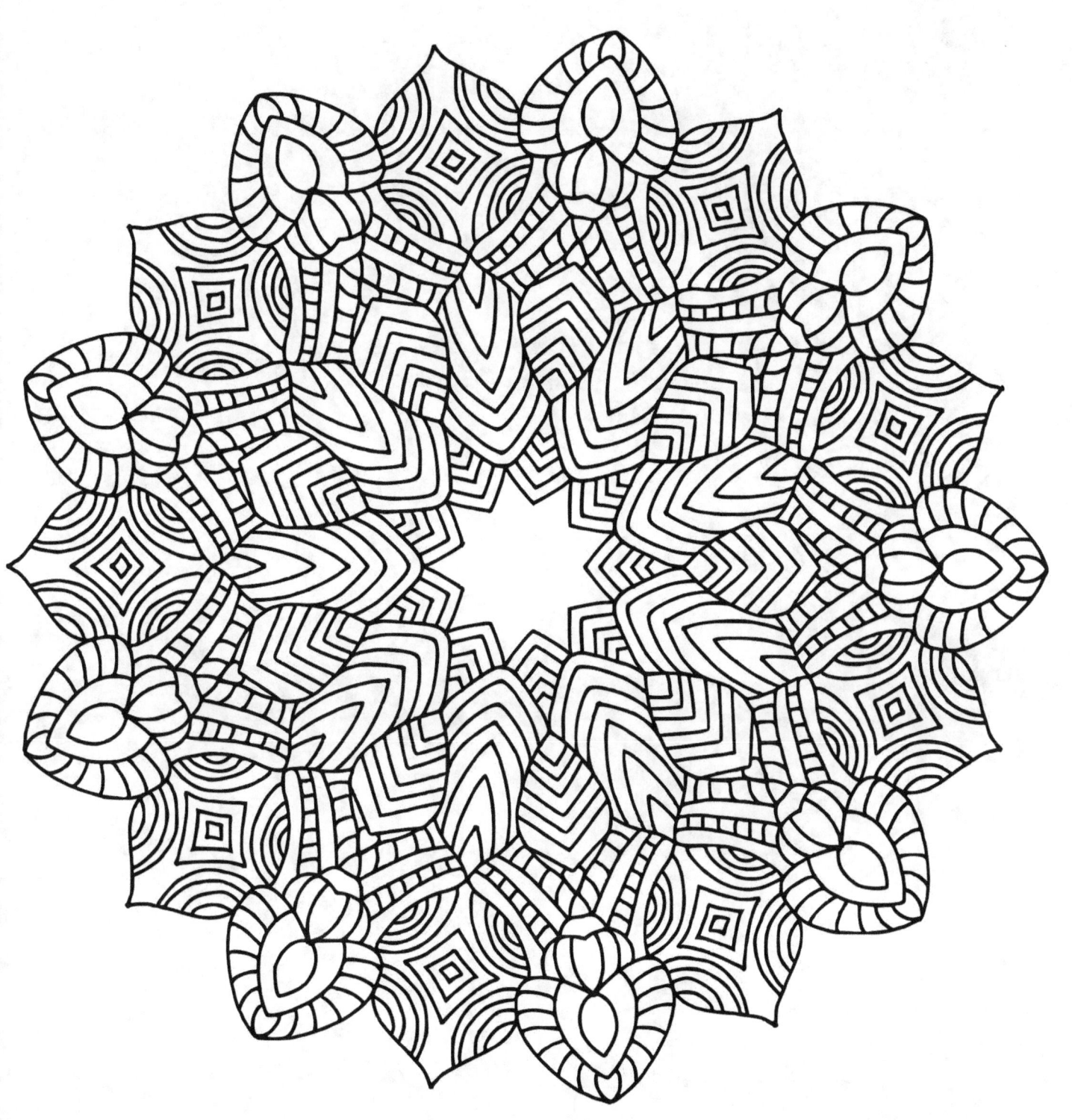

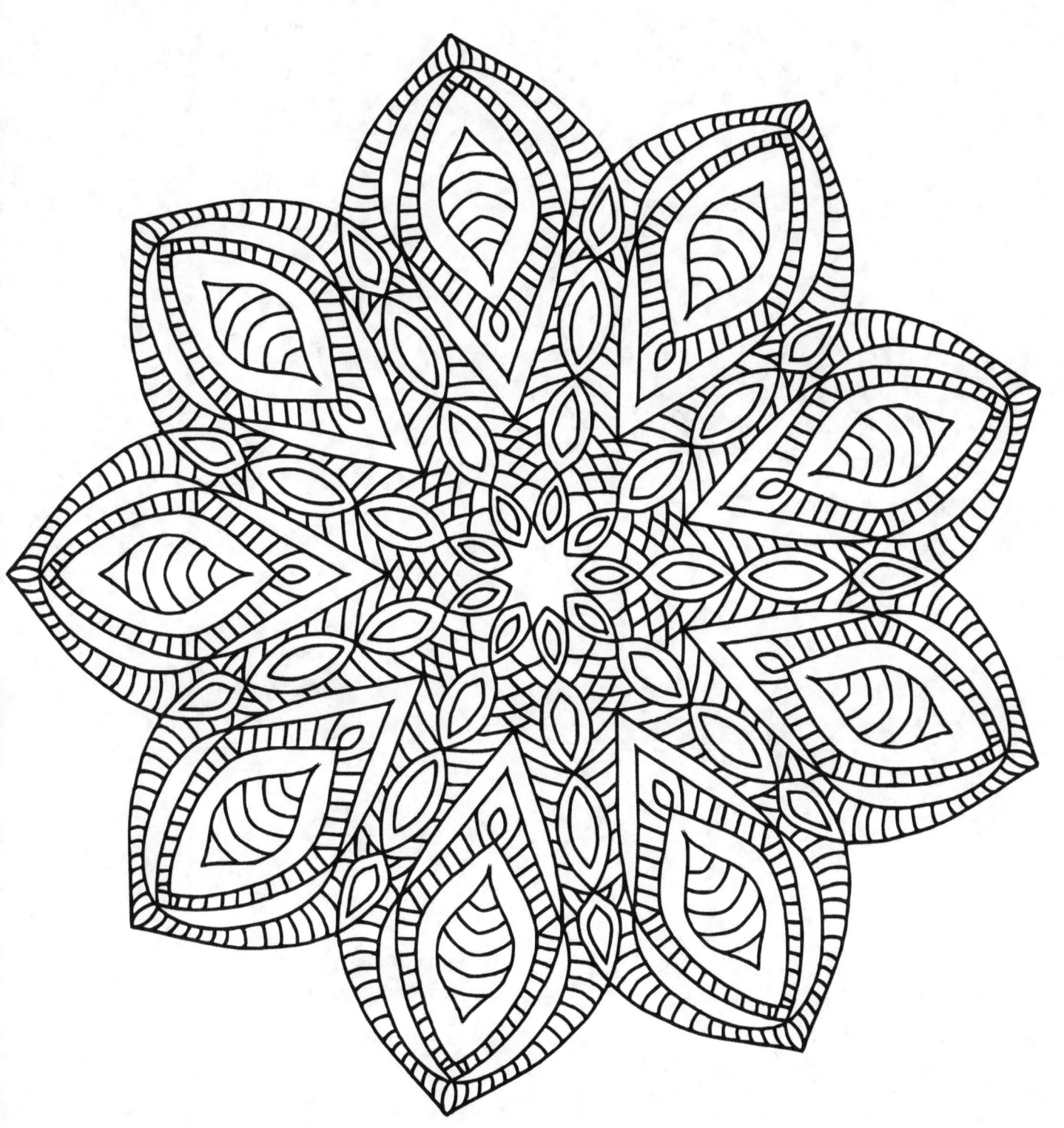

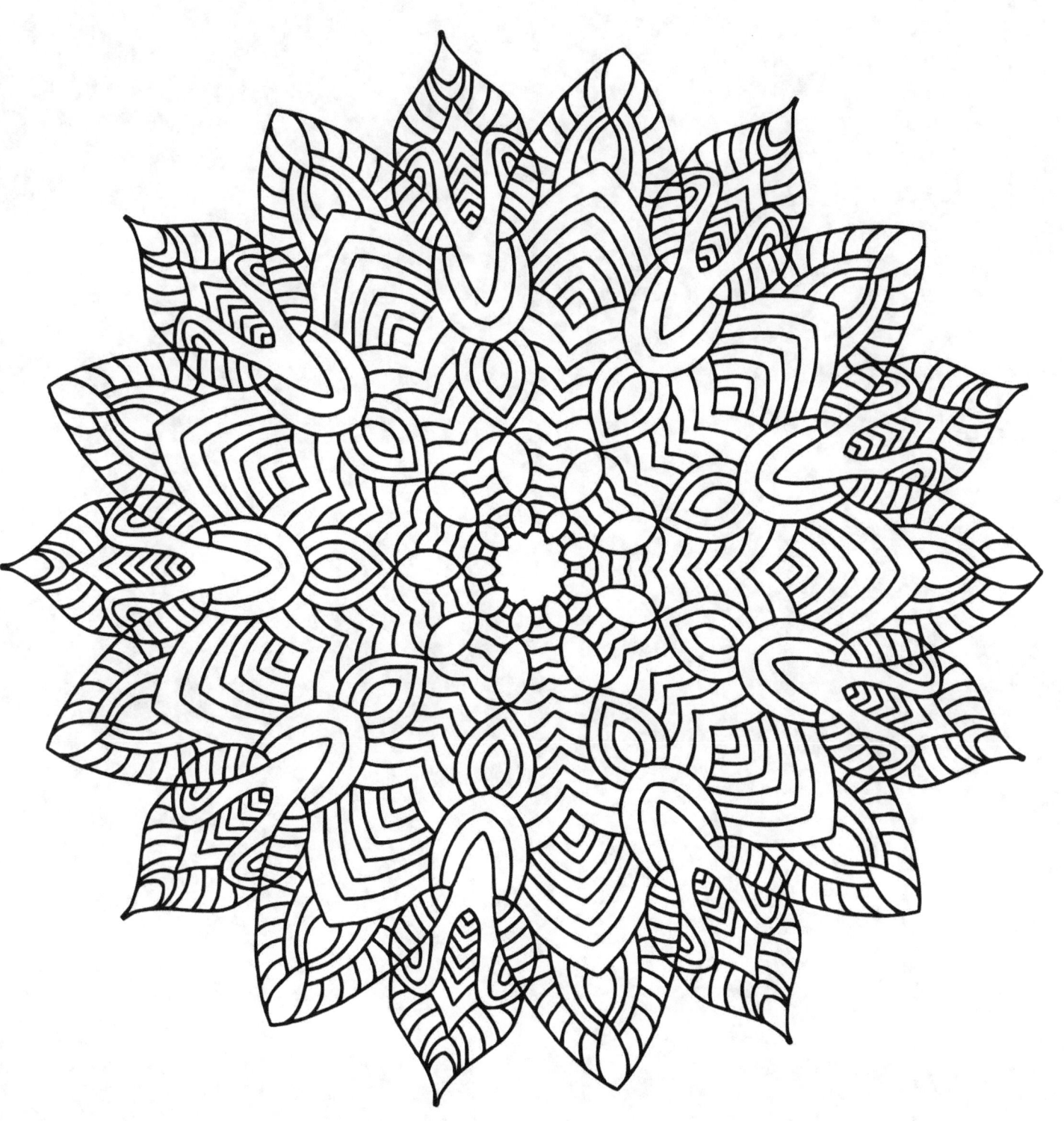

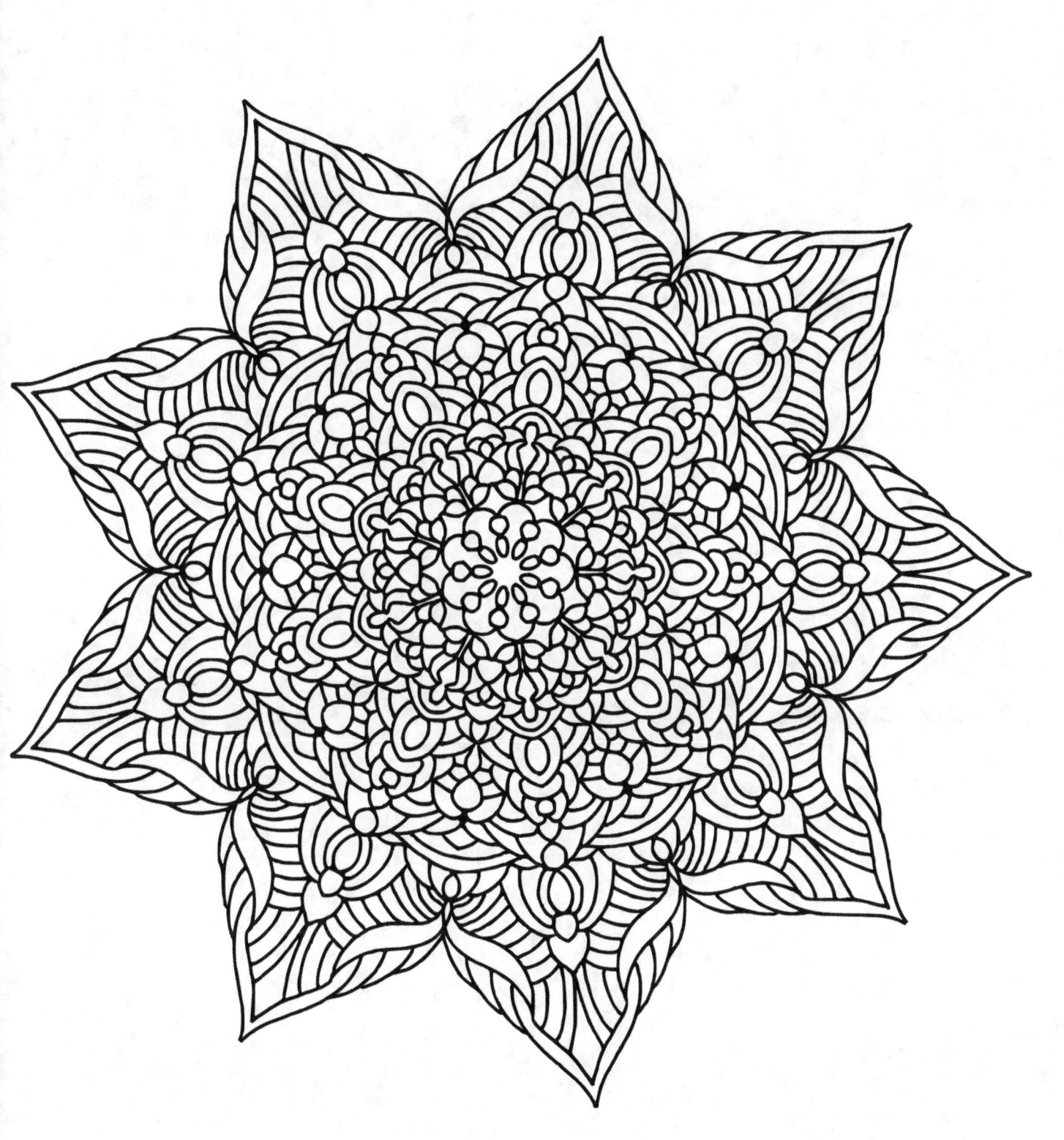

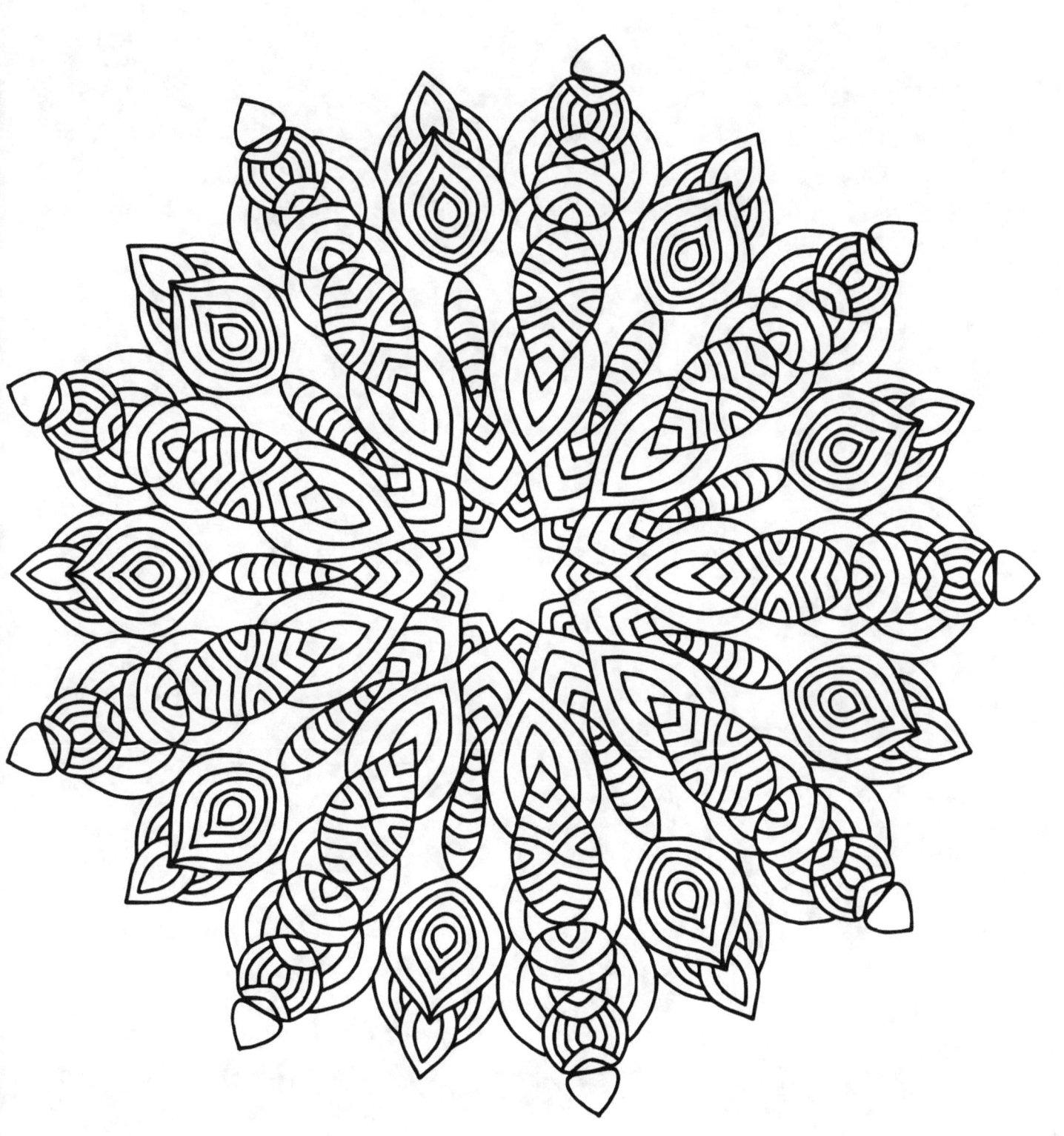

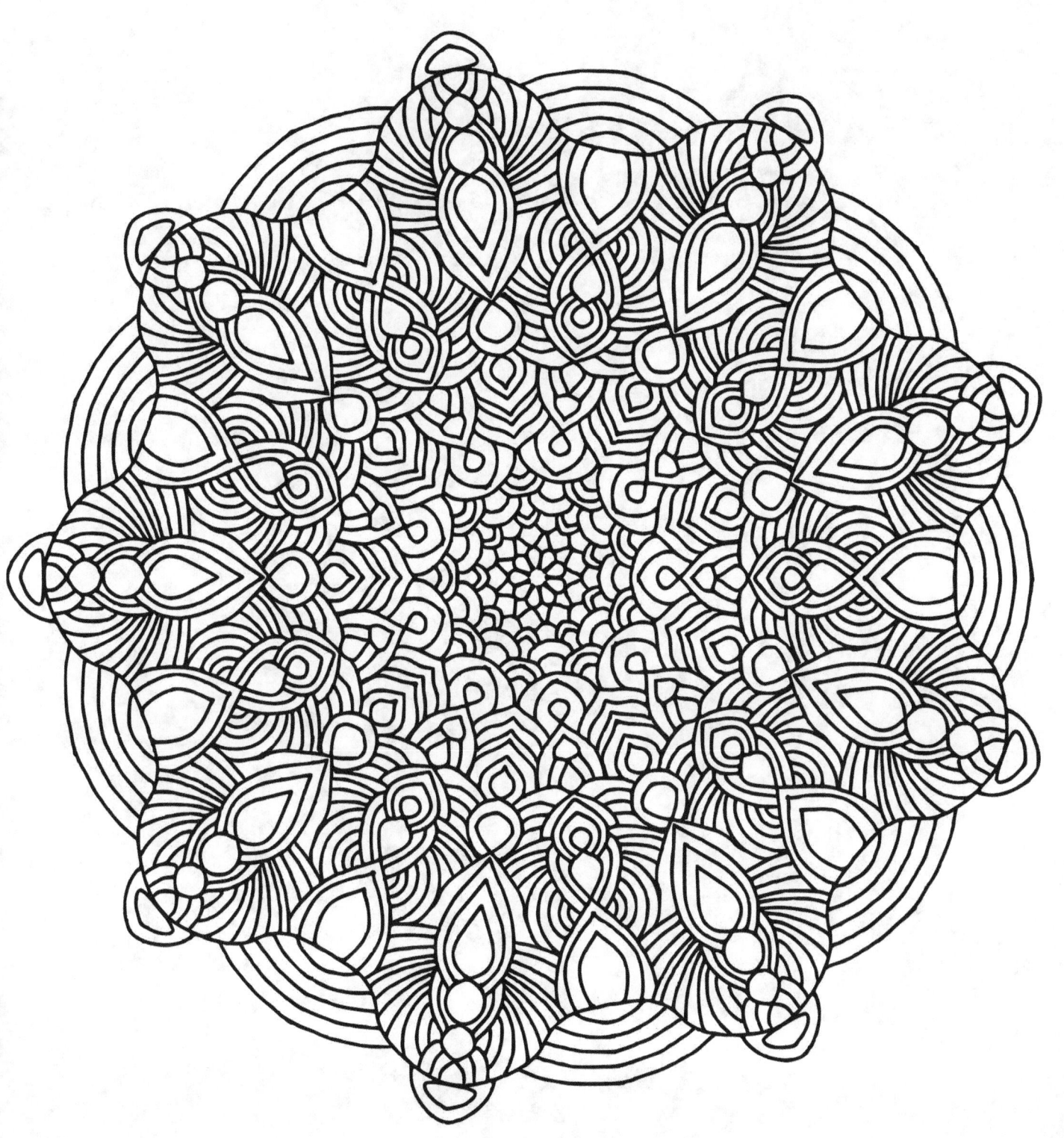

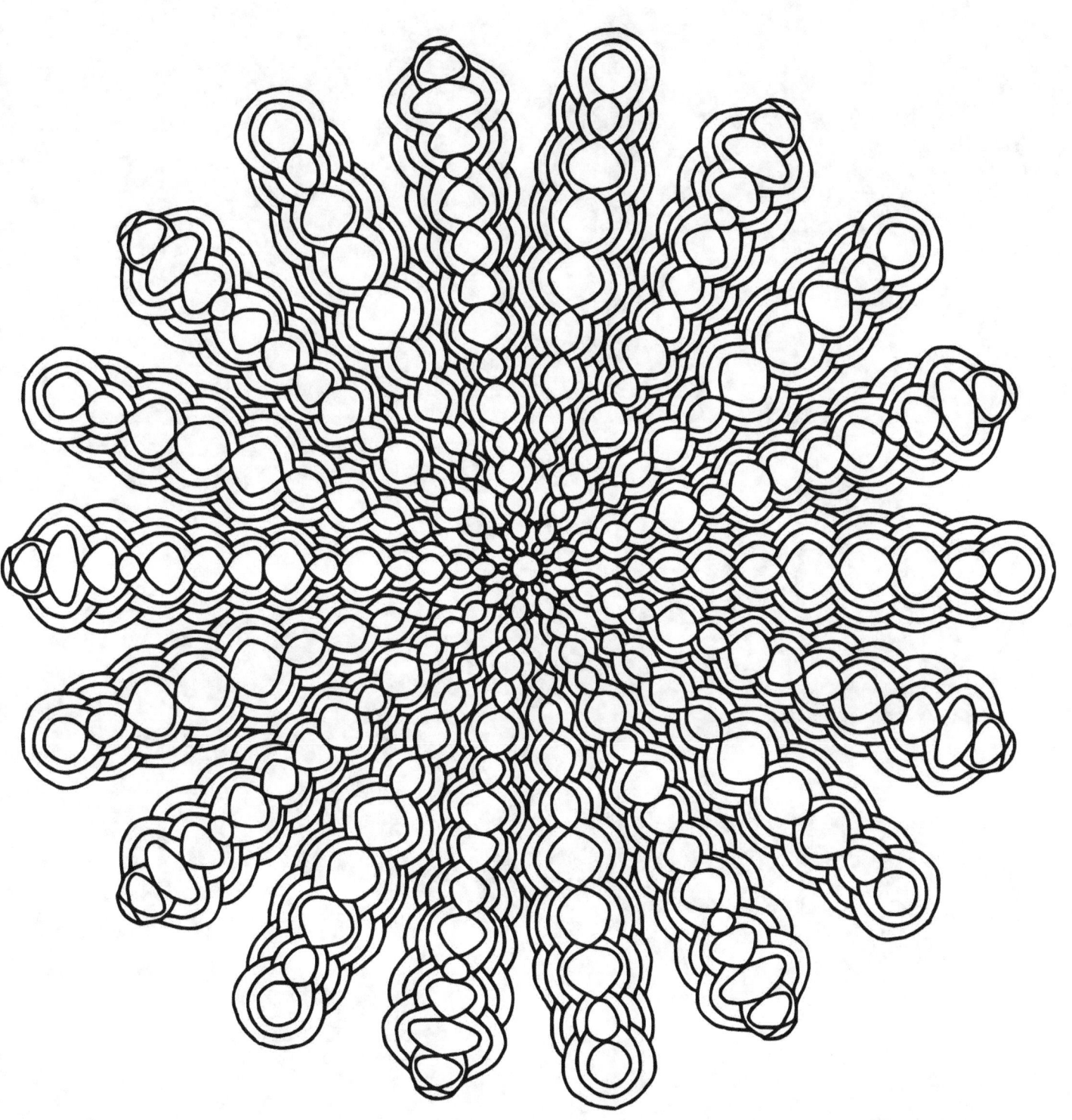

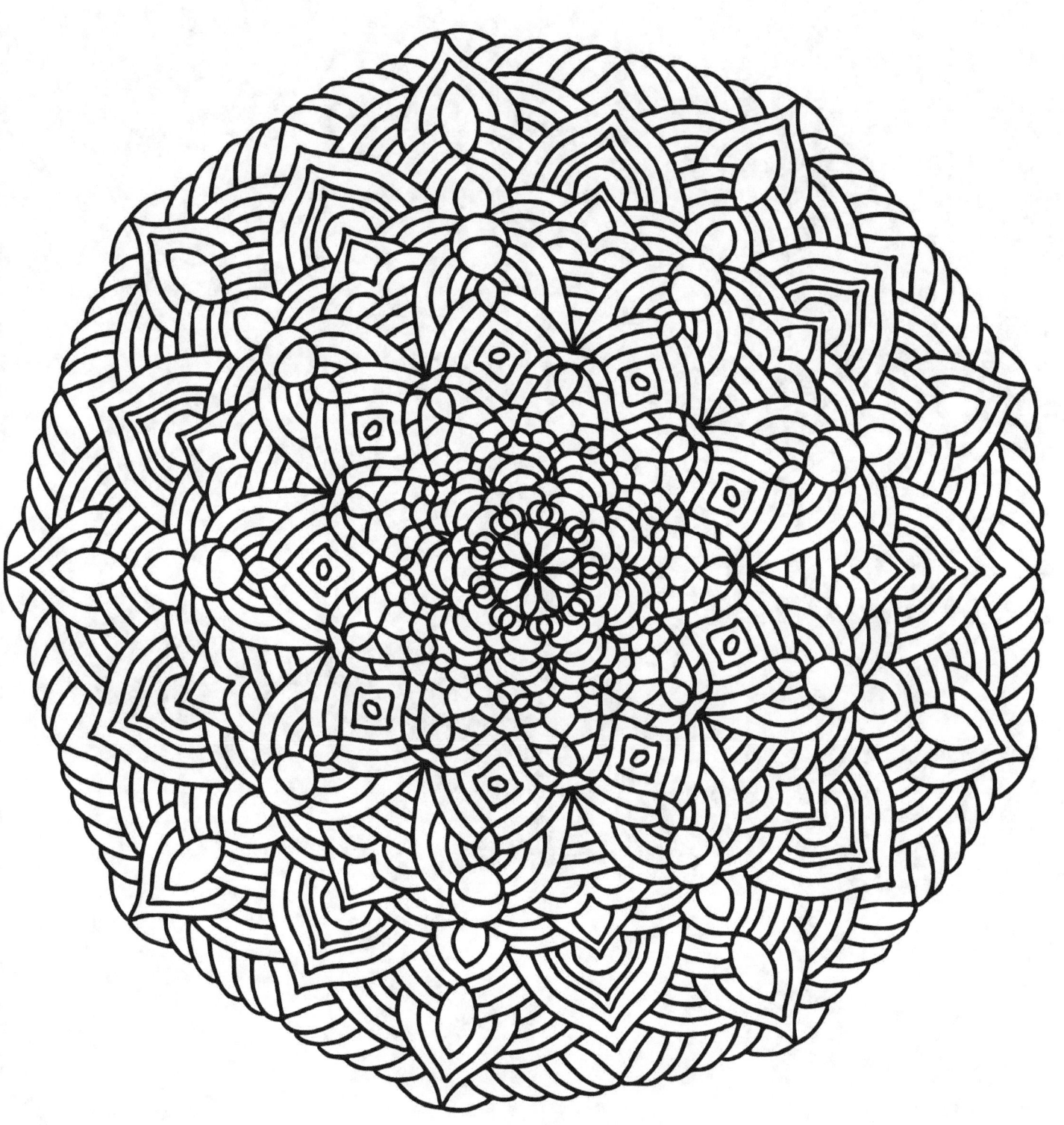

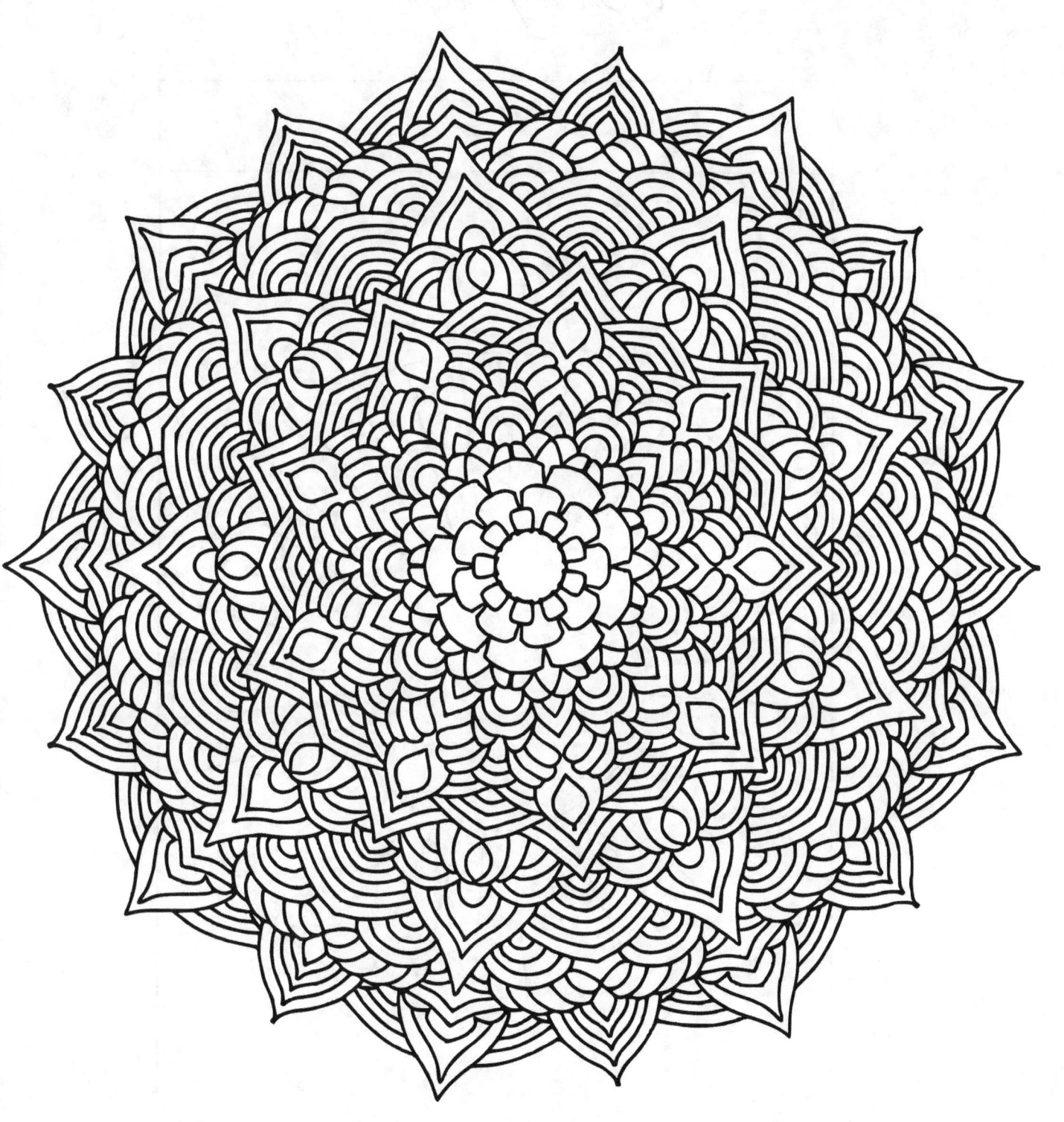

Test your colors here on the samples from
"My Pocket Coloring Companion"
&
"My Coloring Companion"

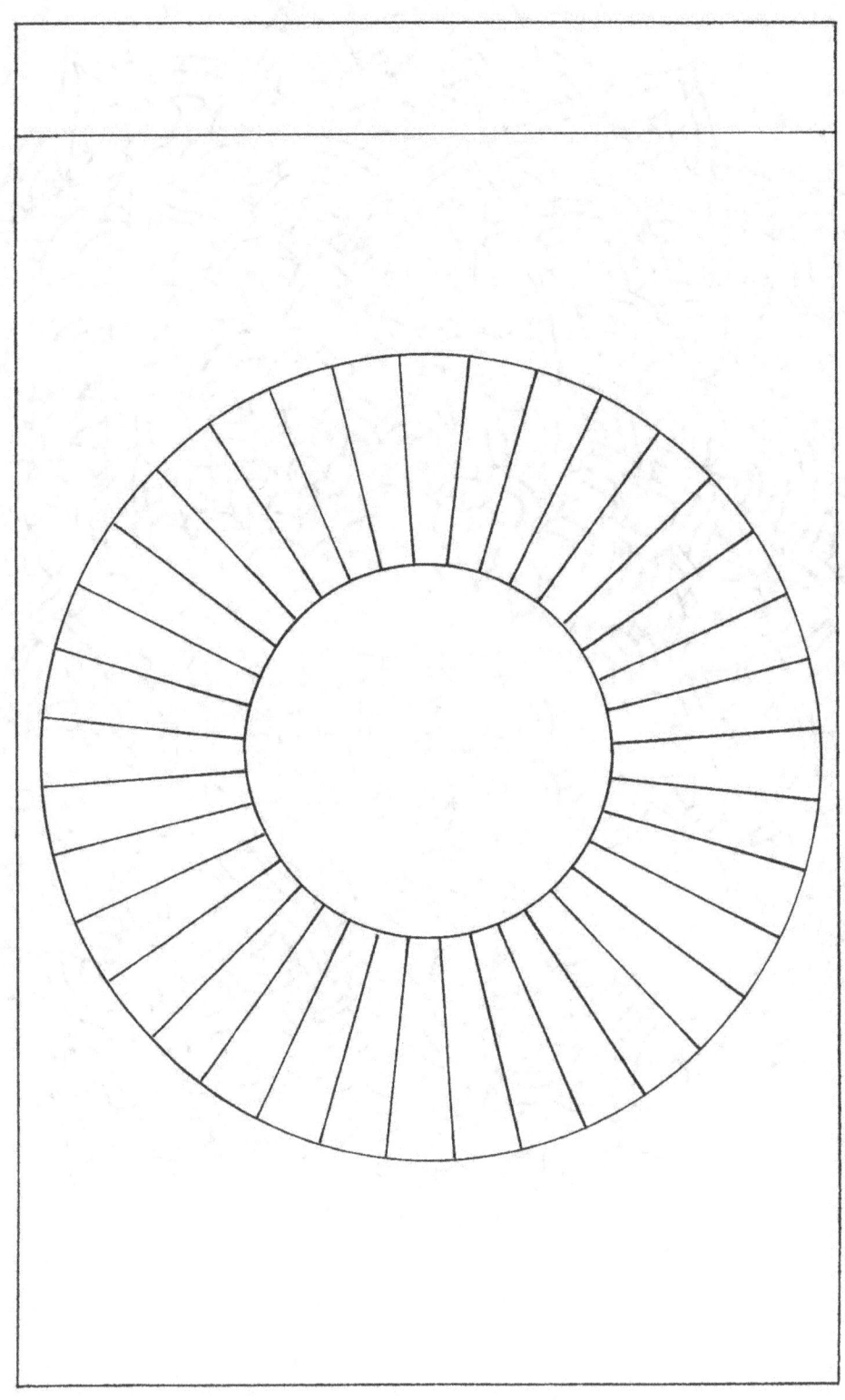

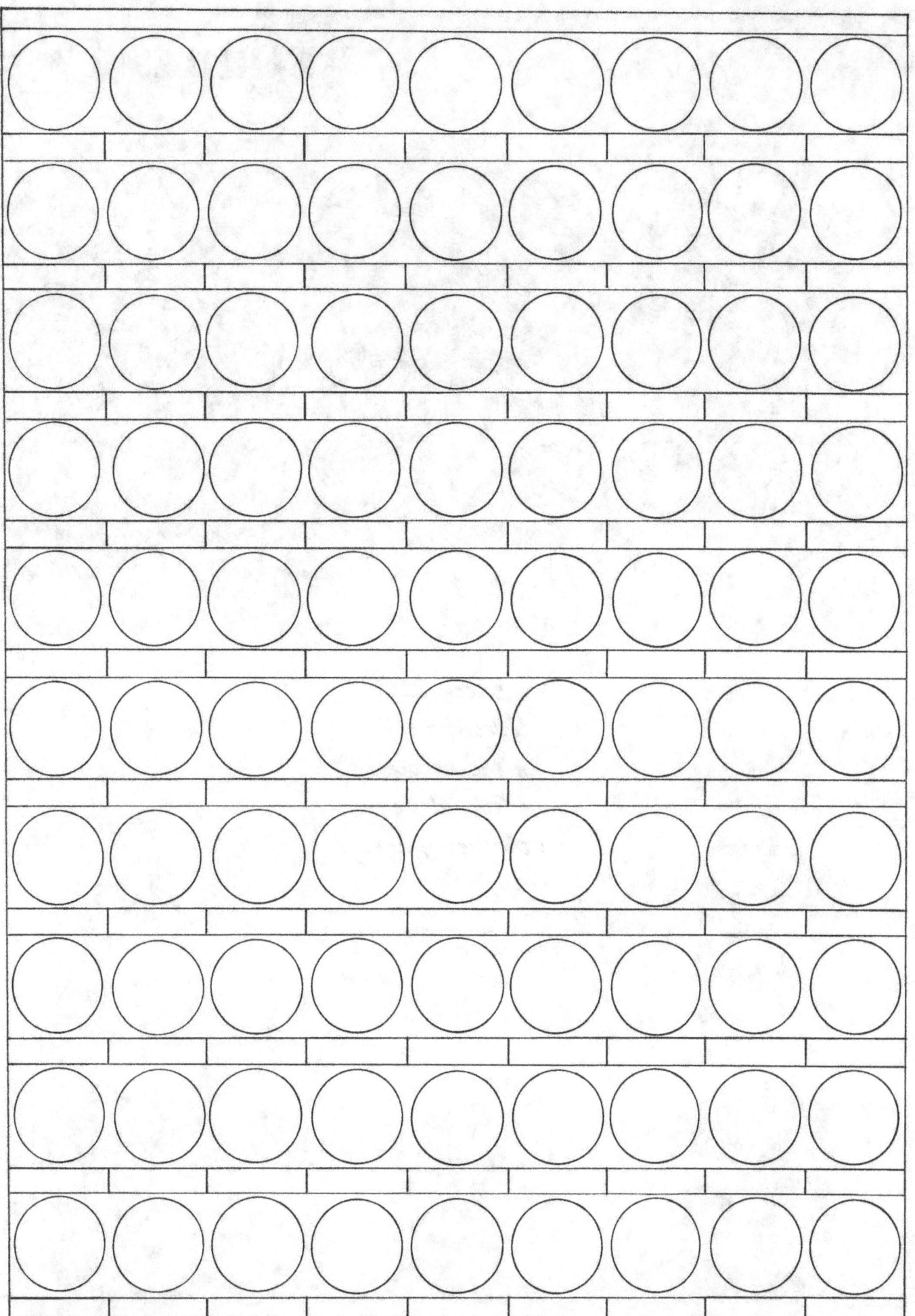

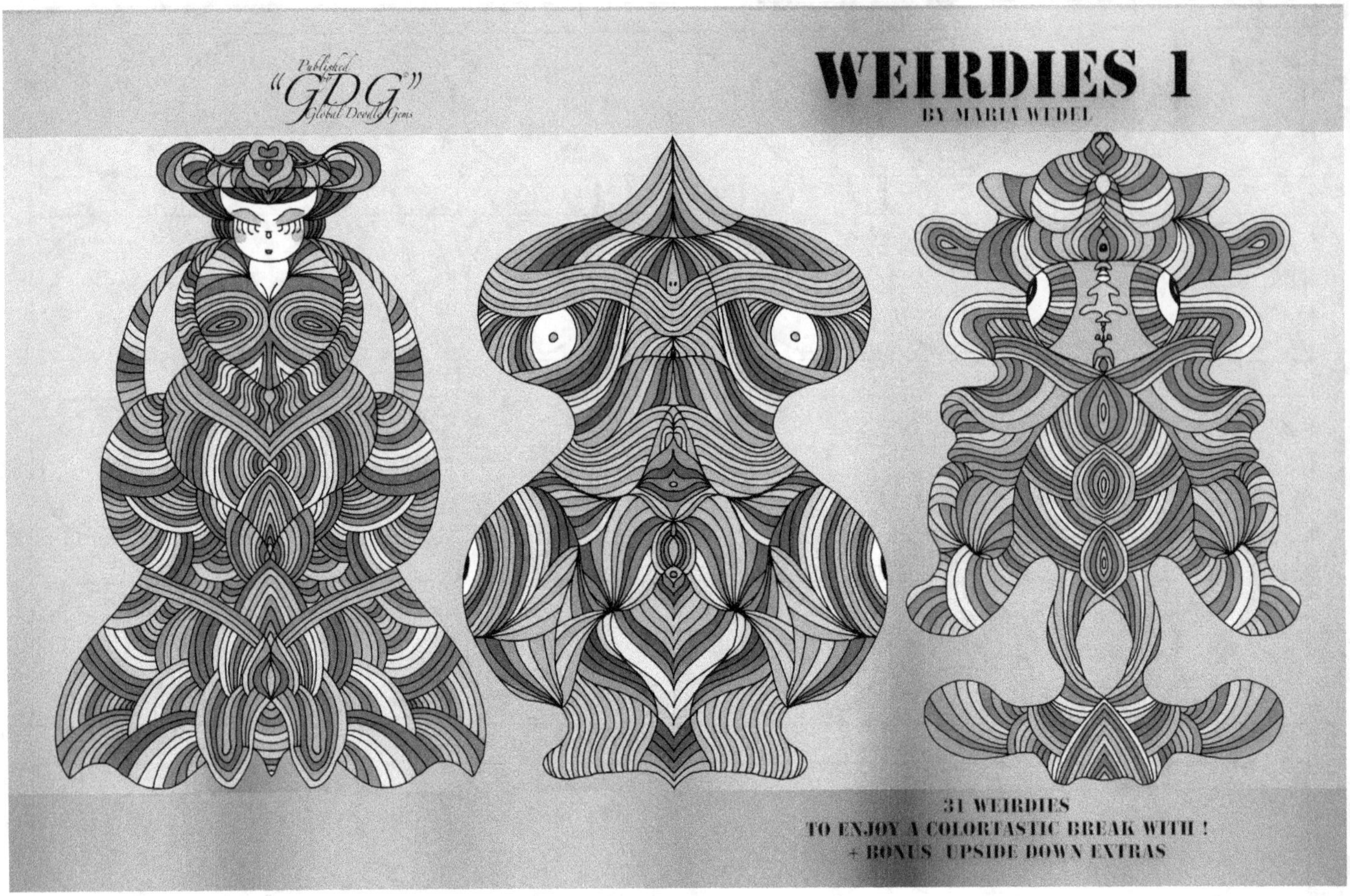

WEIRDIES 1
BY MARIA WEDEL

Published by "GDG" *Global Doodle Gems*

31 WEIRDIES TO ENJOY A COLORTASTIC BREAK WITH ! + BONUS UPSIDE DOWN EXTRAS

Check out Weirdie's 1 in the preview of Weirdie's 1 on the next pages !

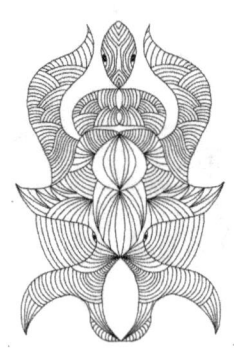
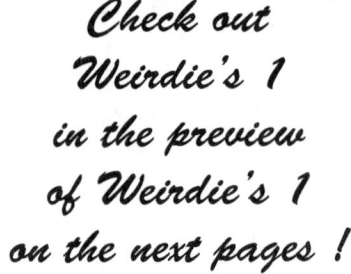
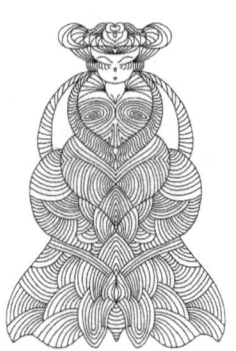
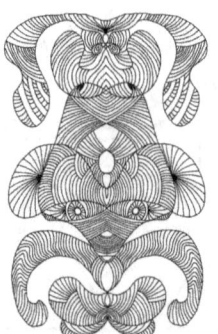
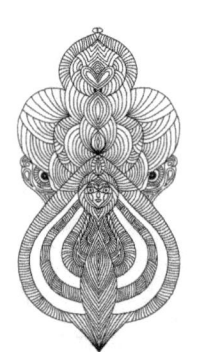
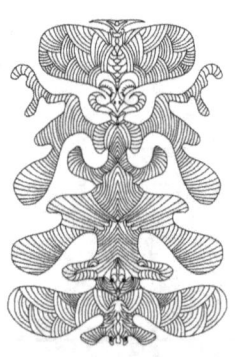

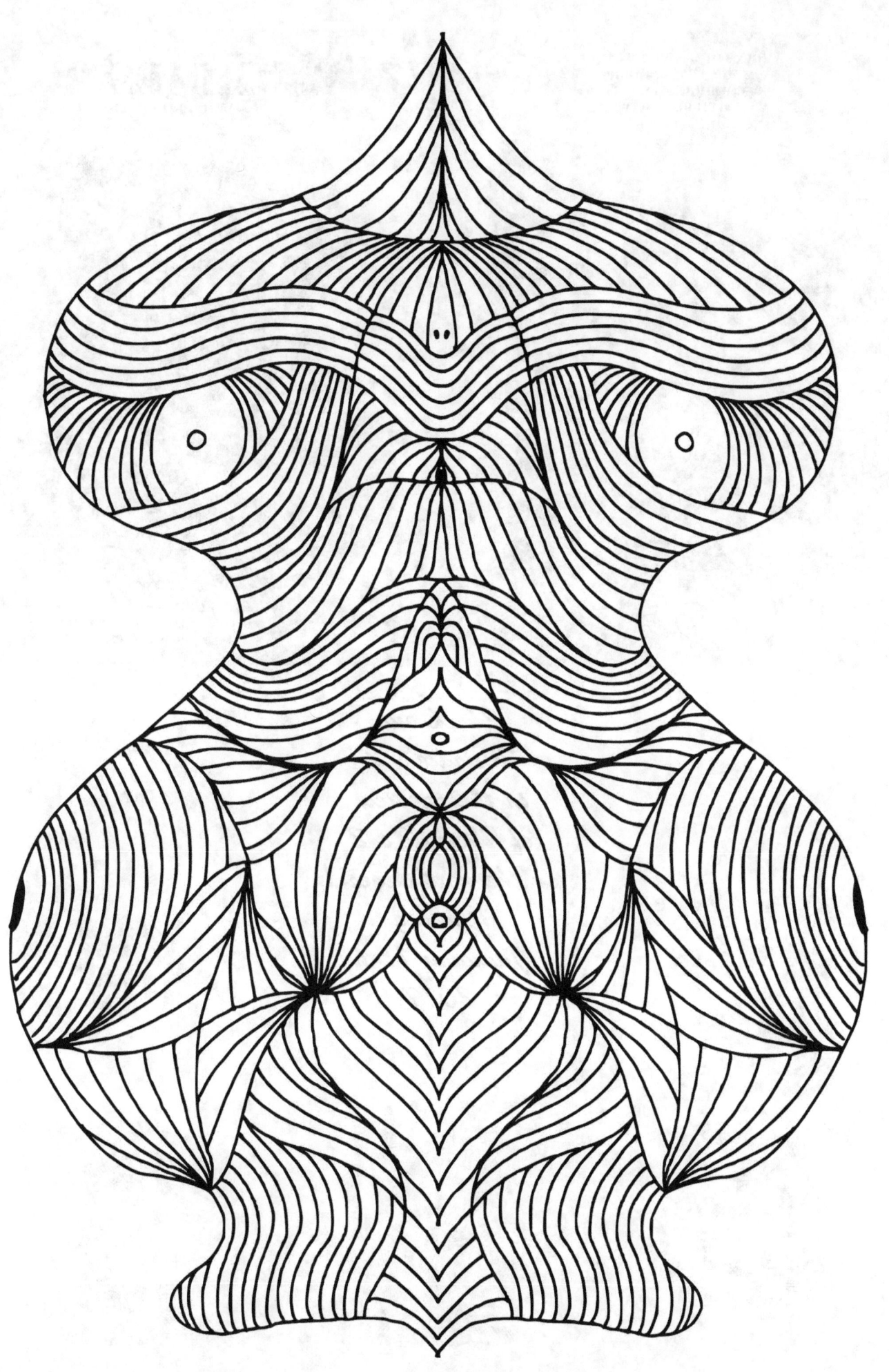

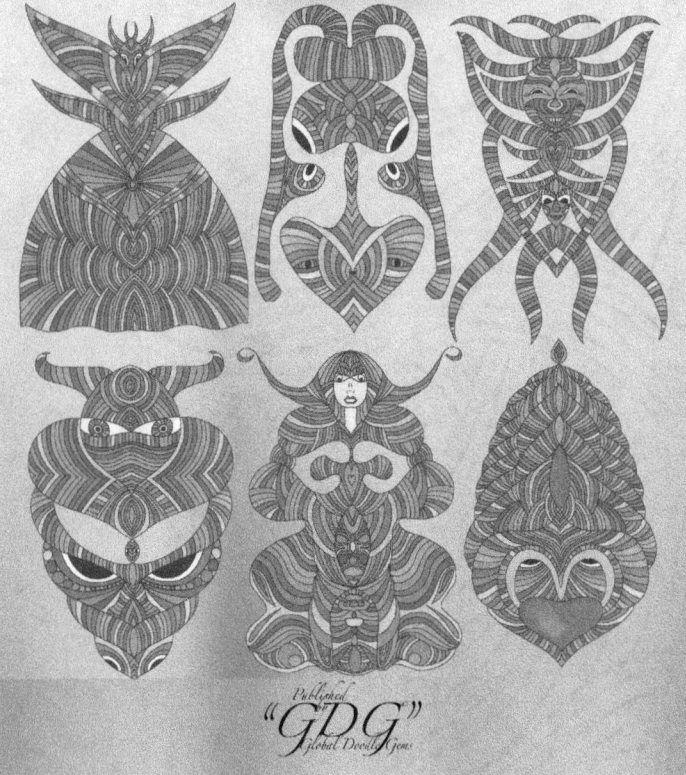
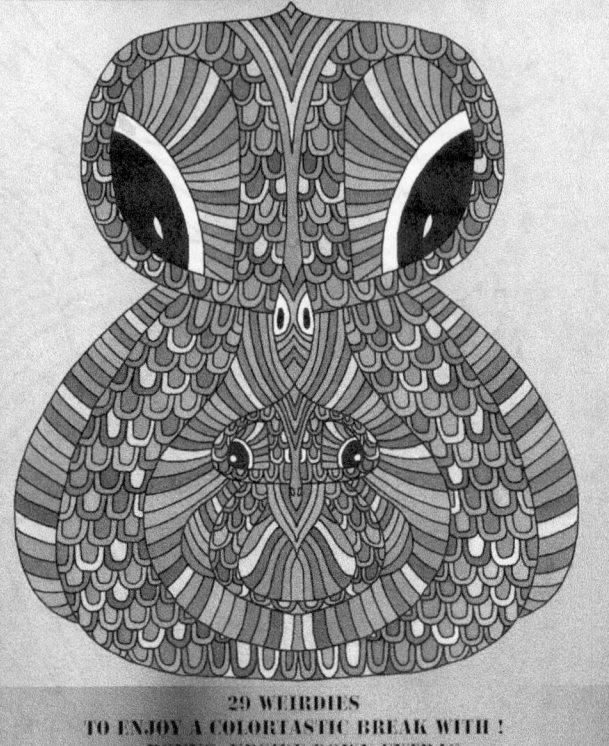

Check out
Weirdie's 2
in the preview
of Weirdie's 2
on the next pages !
Coming
January 15th
2017

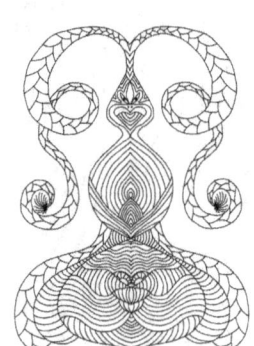
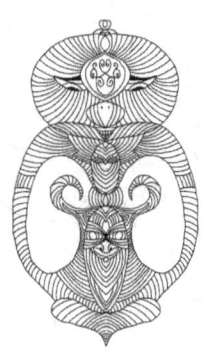
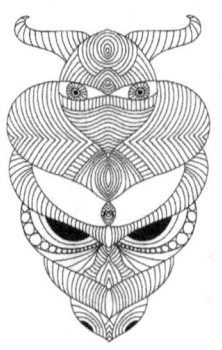
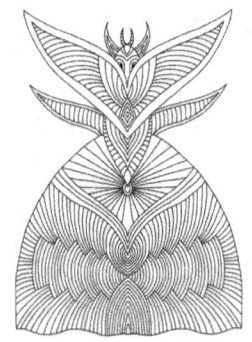
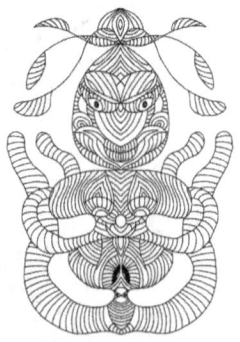

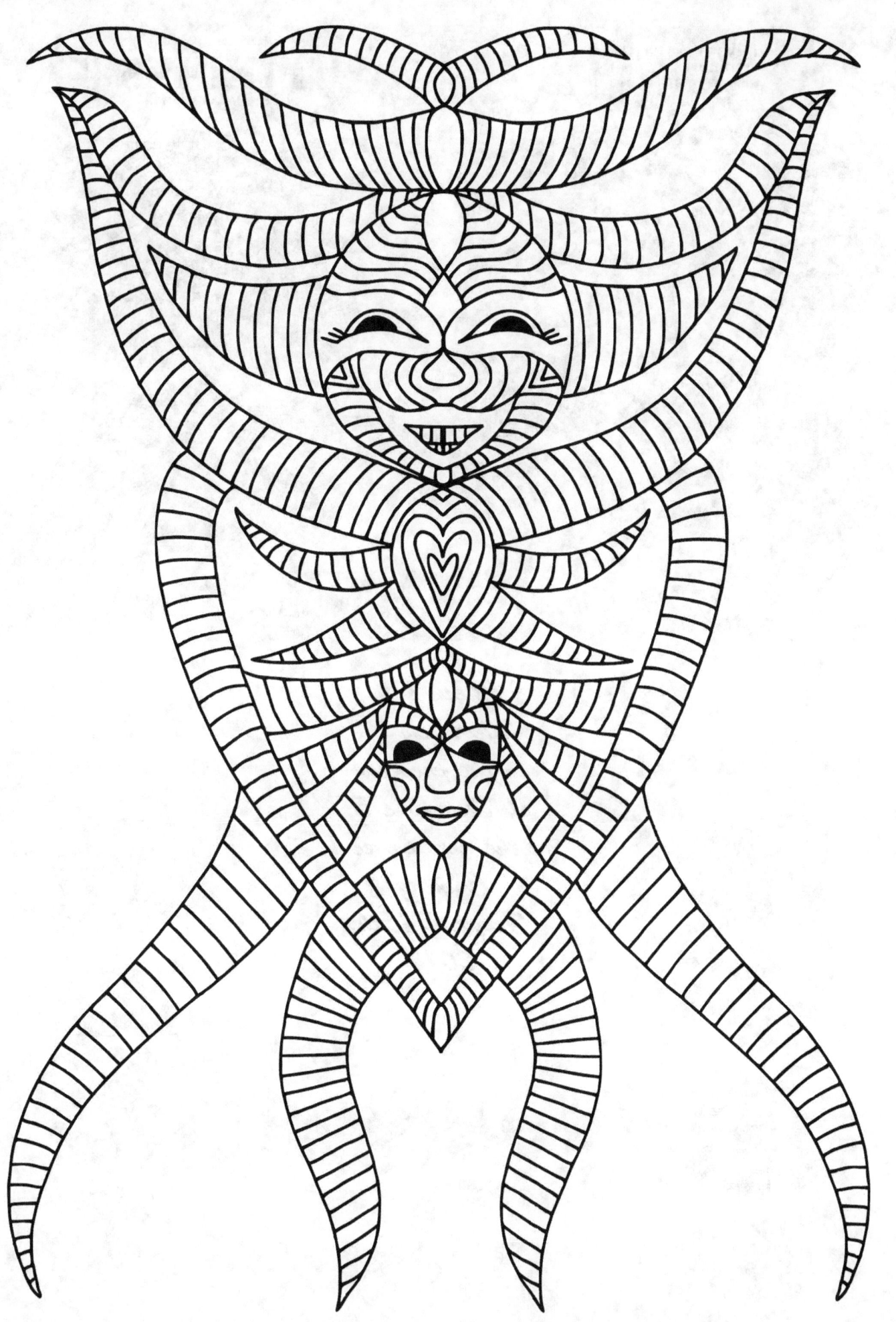

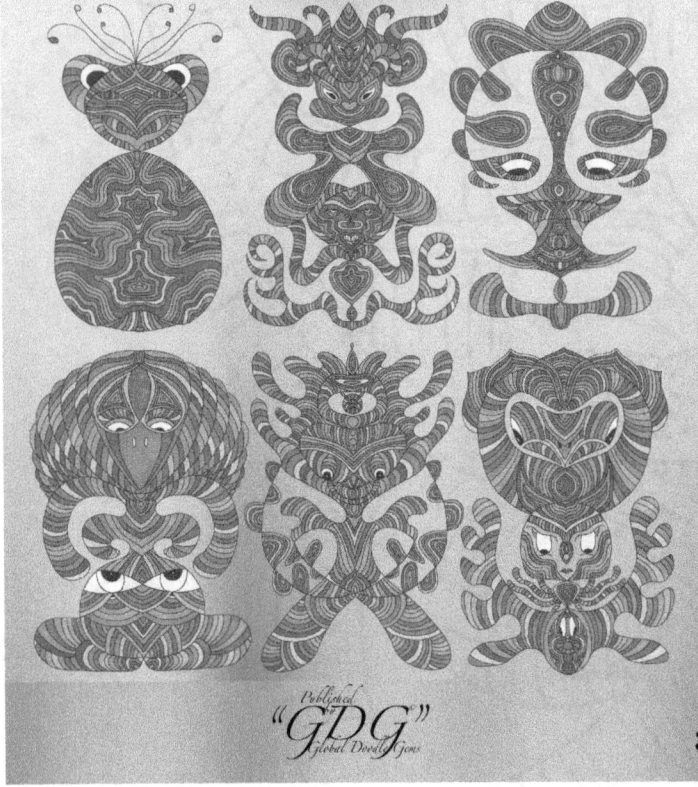
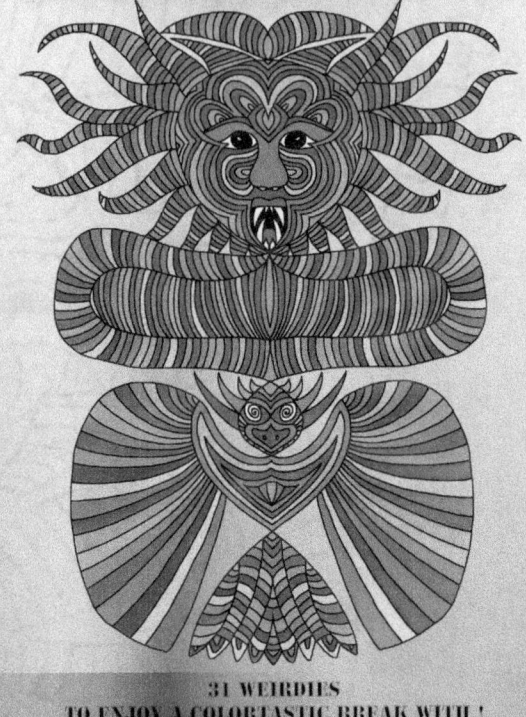

Check out
Weirdie's 3
in the preview
of Weirdie's 3
on the next pages !
Coming
Febuary 15th
2017

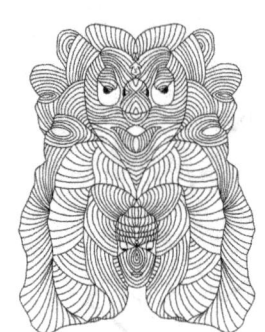
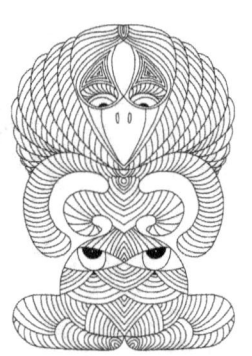
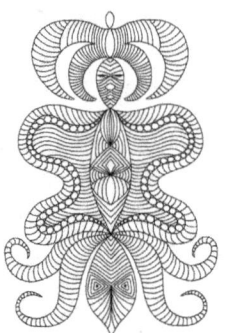
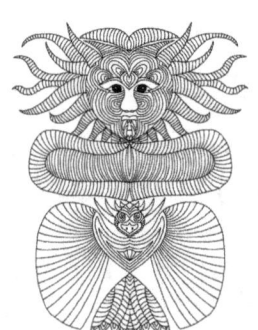
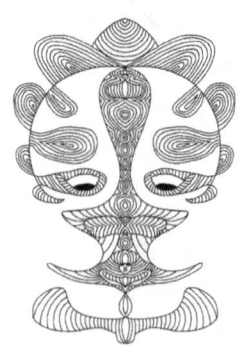

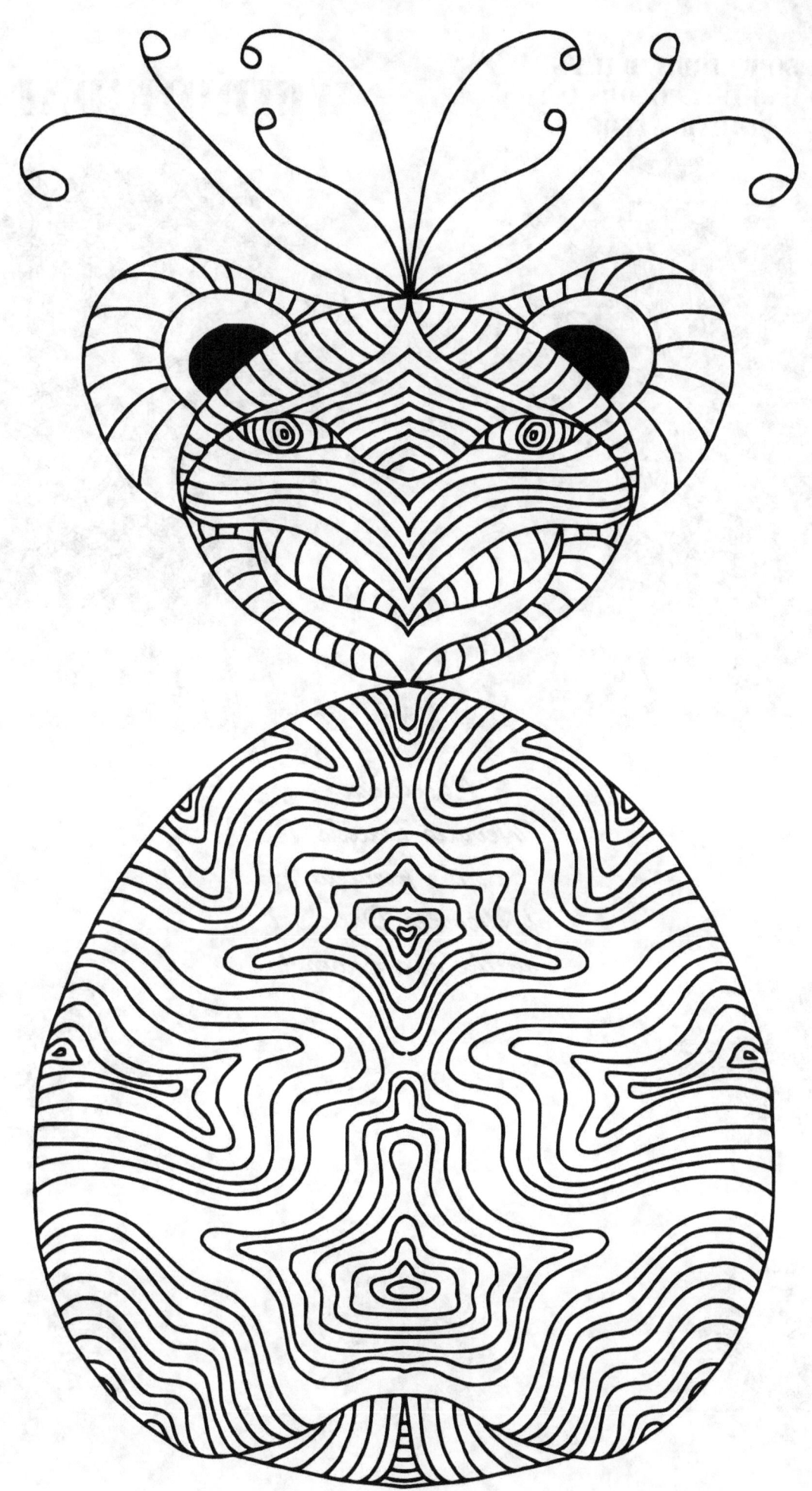

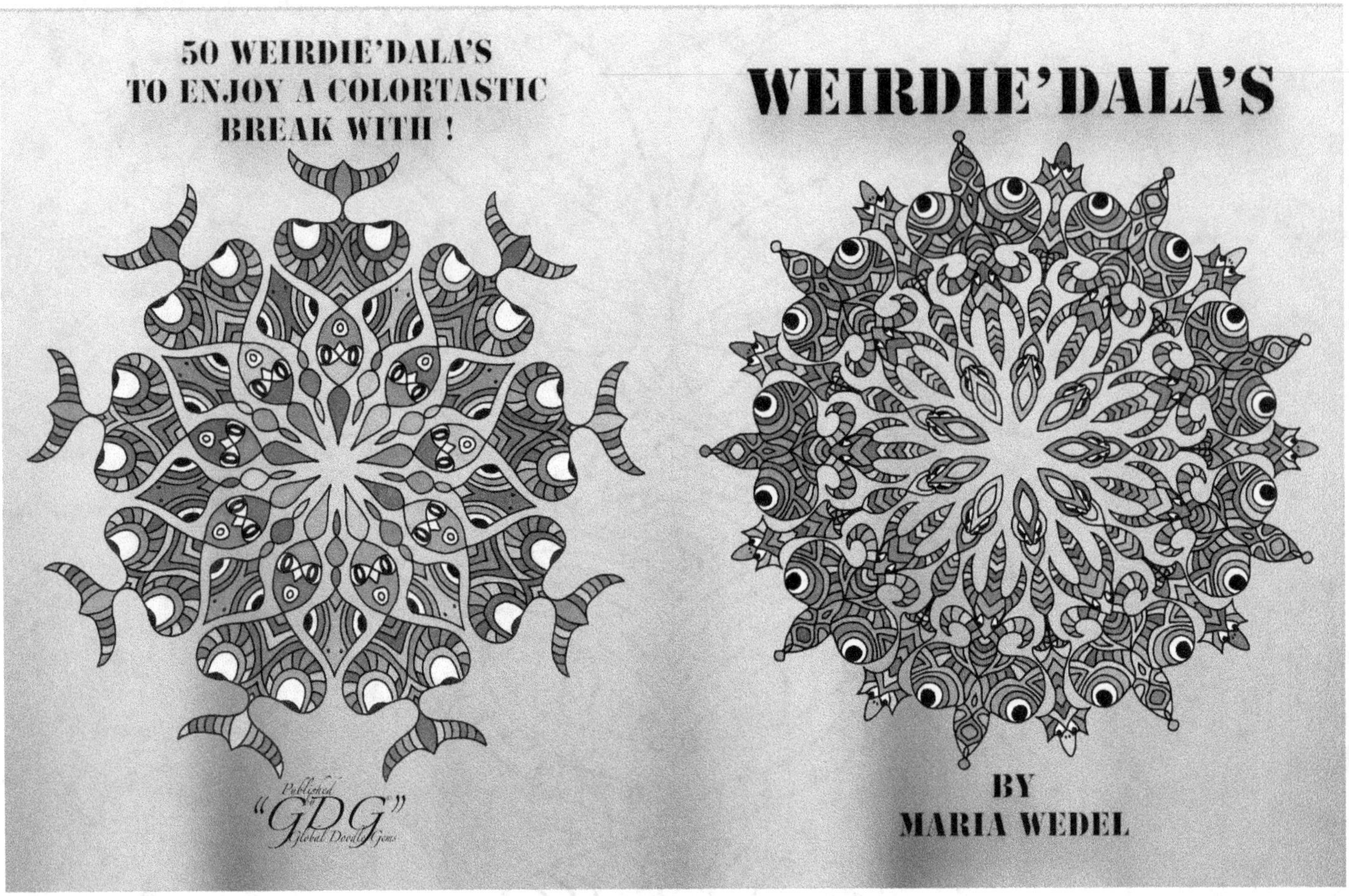

WEIRDIE'DALA'S

50 WEIRDIE'DALA'S TO ENJOY A COLORTASTIC BREAK WITH!

BY MARIA WEDEL

Published "GDG" Global Doodle Gems

*Check out
Weirdie'Dala's 1
in the preview
of Weirdie'Dala's 1
on the next pages !*

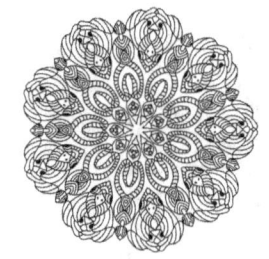
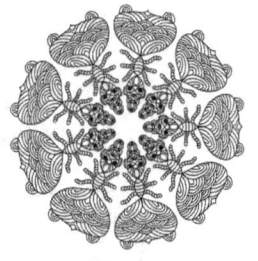
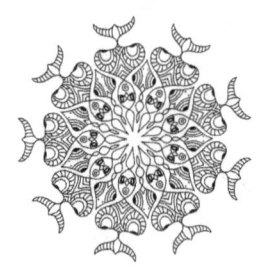
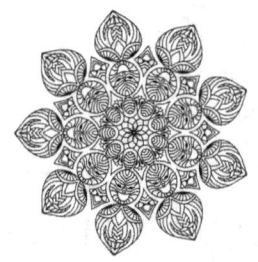
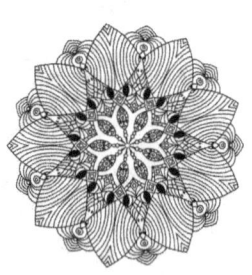

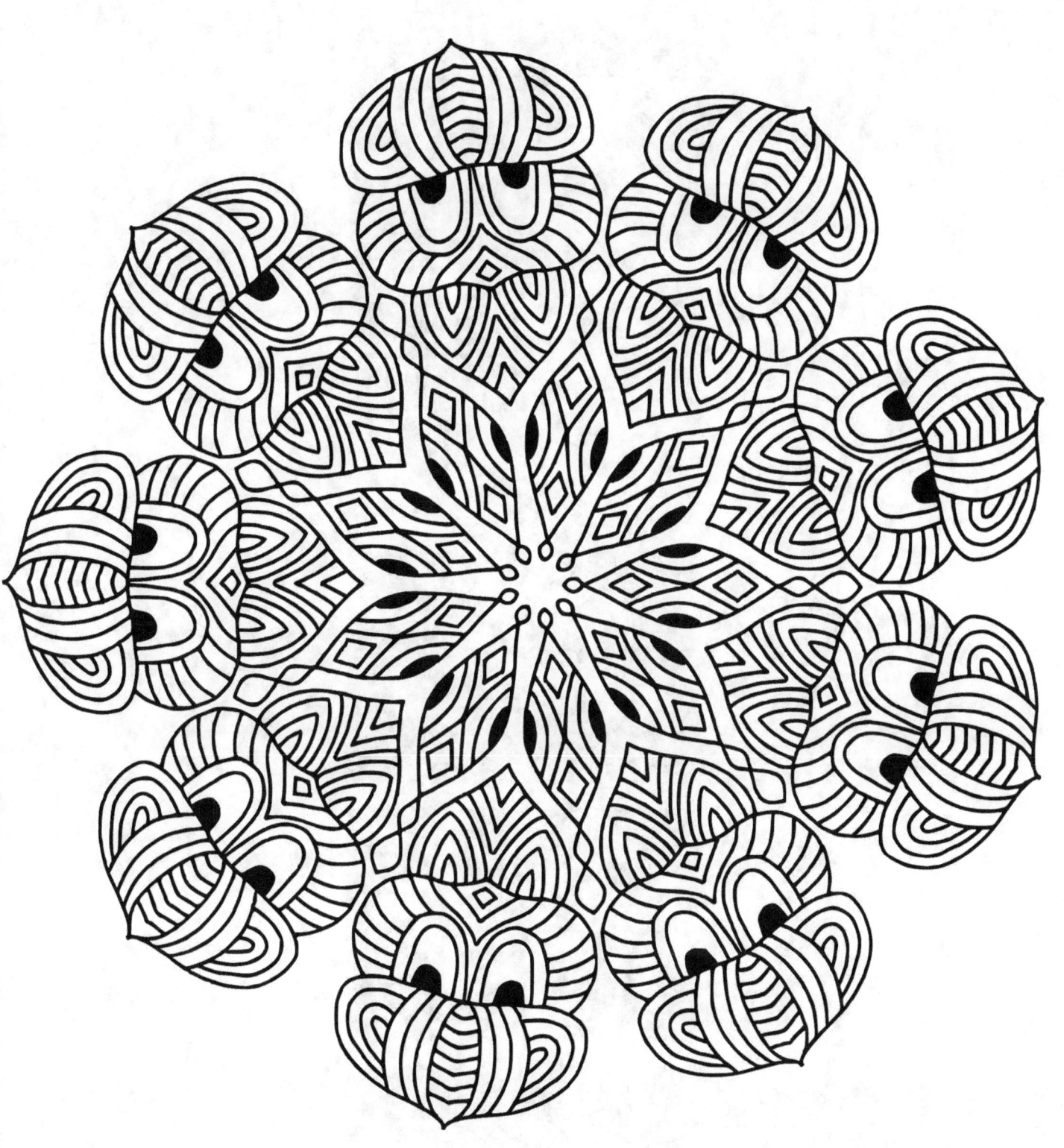

Other Titles by Maria Wedel

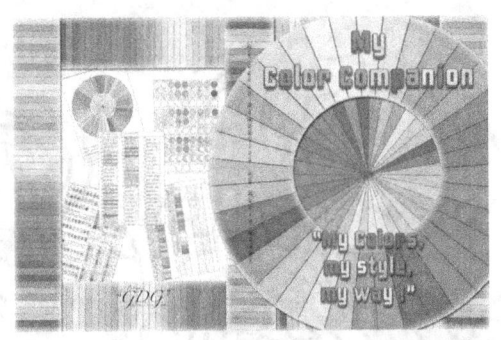
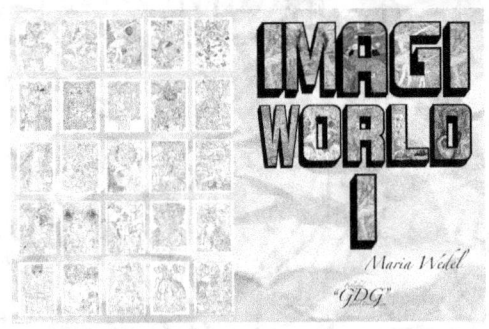
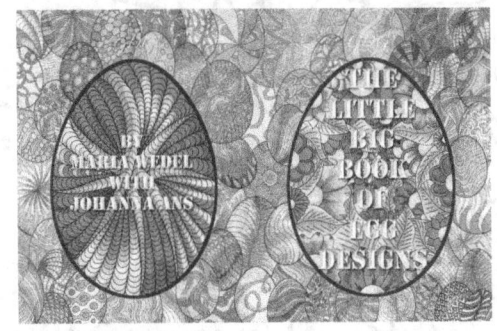
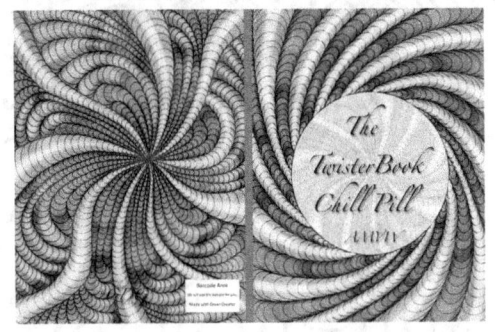
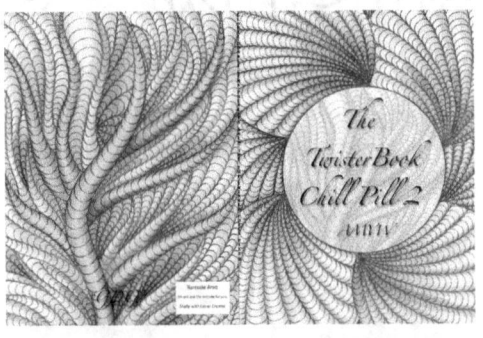

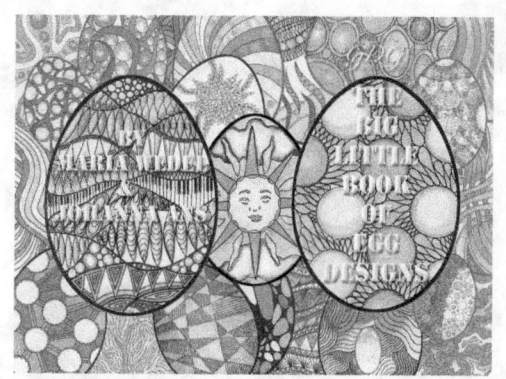
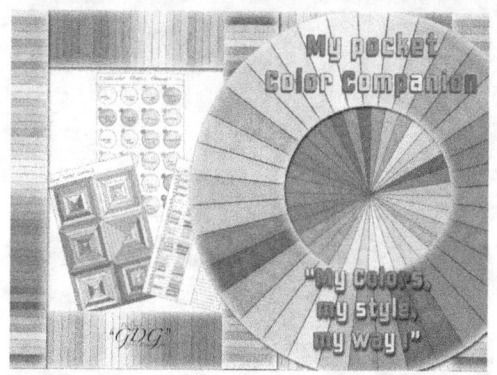
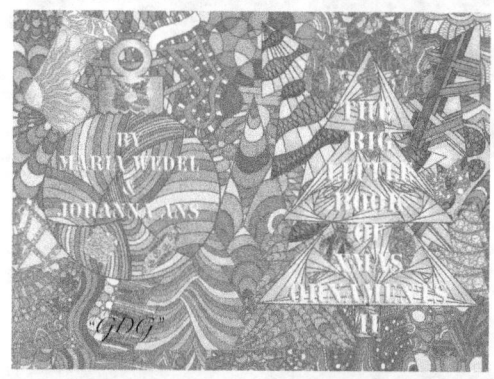
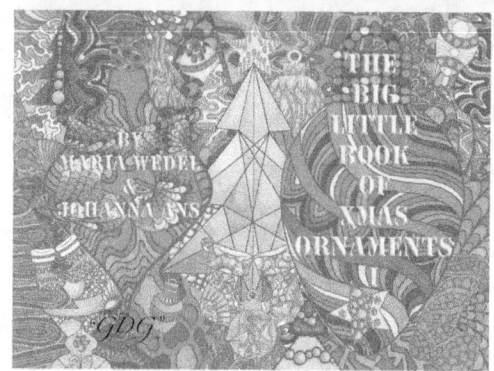
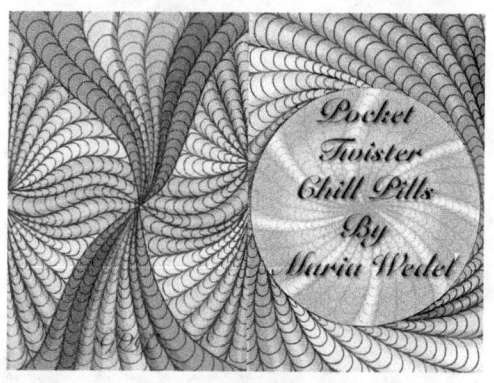